Brilliant As The Sun

A retelling of *Srimad Bhagavatam*
'The Beautiful Science of God'

Canto Eight

Enchanting Pastimes

by

Krishna Dharma
and
Chintamani Dhama Dasi

Copyright © 2022 Krishna Dharma (Kenneth Anderson)

All rights reserved.

ISBN: 9798364742124

DEDICATION

Dedicated to His Divine Grace A.C. Bhaktivedanta Swami Prabhupada, our eternal master. Please cast your merciful glance upon us.

CONTENTS

1	The Universal Administrators	1
2	Gajendra's Dilemma	5
3	Gajendra Liberated	9
4	Gajendra's Past Life	15
5	The Gods Cursed	20
6	The Truce	33
7	Shiva Drinks Poison	41
8	Churning the Milk Ocean	50
9	Vishnu Becomes a Woman	59
10	The Battle	67
11	Indra Destroys the Asuras	74
12	Lord Shiva Bewildered	81
13	The Manus	88
14	The Cosmic Administration	91
15	The Great King Bali	94
16	Sage Kashyapa Instructs Aditi	103
17	Aditi Sees Lord Vishnu	112
18	The Divine Dwarf	116
19	Vamana Begs Charity	121
20	Bali Surrenders the Universe	131
21	Bali Arrested	139
22	Bali Surrenders	145
23	The Heavens Regained	154
24	Matsya the Divine Fish	162
	Appendices	174
	Notes	187
	Glossary	203
	About the Authors	208
	Other Titles in the Series	209

Foreword

The Srimad Bhagavatam's eighth canto is aptly called "enchanting pastimes." In this retelling by Krishna Dharma and Chintamani Dhama Dasi in their *Brilliant as the Sun* series, anyone can easily experience this divine enchantment. Shukadeva Goswami's narrative of the various Manus (universal administrators), and the incarnations of the Lord who appear at different times, leads to the story of Gajendra, literally "Elephant King." Even for those who know this story well, the way the narrative unfolds in this retelling draws us into the emotions and realisations of the divine personalities. The Lord's benediction about remembering the persons, the place, and the events become so much easier when we read it in this flowing story form.

Then we enter the main narrative of the eighth canto, which moves through Indra's pride and subsequent defeat by the Asuras, to the famous story of the milk ocean churning and the battle there, and then again Indra's defeat by Bali, and then to Bali's defeat by Vamana that puts Indra back, yet again, in charge of the heavens.

In that story of intergalactic intrigue, arrogance, humility, greed, battles, deception, and strategy, we find some of the most amazing incarnations of Lord Vishnu. He helps carry the great golden mountain and heal the gods crushed under its weight. He calls for Vasuki as a churning rope. He comes as the unfathomably great turtle who holds up the mountain in the milk ocean. The Lord, as a turtle, has his back scratched and his ornaments polished as Mandara Mountain moves back and forth in the churning. His breath moves with the tides as he is the base of the pivot between the pious and the evil, both of whom he facilitates. The Lord also stays on top of the mountain with uncountable arms. From that ocean come treasures, animals, and some of the most significant personalities in the universe, including the goddess of fortune. When she chooses Lord Vishnu as her spouse, she delivers profound instructions about the relative value and character of anyone other than the Lord as our most beloved.

The result of the churning is not just all the wondrous beings who emerge from the milk but also the Lord himself, as Dhanvantari, master of medicine. He holds the nectar that is the goal of the ocean churning, which awards long, healthy life to those who drink it and empowers one with extraordinary strength. Although he is the Lord, the Asuras take the nectar from him, thus threatening to skew the universal balance of good and evil.

At this point, the Lord incarnates most fascinatingly as the supremely attractive female. Although the scriptures generally describe the Supreme Lord as the ultimate male, they also describe him as the complete whole, the source of everything. Such an understanding includes that the Supreme is also the perfection of femininity. And what a woman! Mohini uses her supernatural charms to insert a plot twist that moves the pastime from a truce to share the nectar between the warring parties to a strategy of trickery and victory for the gods.

When the Asuras shake off their enchantment, there is a universal conflict of epic proportions. The ferocious battle gradually brings us back to the effort of Bali's Asura army to take over the universe. After being slain in combat, Bali is resurrected by his guru's mystic power, and is finally able to conquer Indra. This time Vishnu intervenes with a different type of subterfuge in response to the prayers and austerities of Indra's mother, Aditi. Appearing as Indra's younger brother in the form of a dwarf, the Lord charms Bali into giving away the entire universe and his very self as a loving donation of service. Bali thus becomes celebrated as the epitome of surrender. The relationship between Bali and Vamana is full of twists and turns of loving sweetness, bringing about a transformation in our hearts. There is a bonus, too—the description of the universe as God's body. This description was also found in the *Bhagavatam's* second canto, and here again, we discover how to find God in the daily life of what we see, hear, smell, and touch in the world.

After completing the complex story of the gods and Asuras in their struggle for universal control, and the role of the Lord in many forms in that struggle, the eighth canto ends with yet another fabulous incarnation of God—as a fish named Matsya. This story has parallels with those in other religions and cultures, telling of a worldwide flood, where the Lord saves a faithful few, along with the means of restoring the Earth after the flood. The charming relationship between the Lord as Matsya and the king serving him is profoundly inspiring and uplifting.

So, melt your heart with these charming pastimes of the beautiful Bhagavatam, as brilliant as the sun, in this accessible, deep, and delightful retelling.

Urmila devi dasi (Dr. Edith Best)
Author of *Essence Seekers* and *The Great Mantra for Mystic Meditation*

Introduction

We have reached the eighth canto in our retelling of *Srimad Bhagavatam*. Those who have been with us on the journey will know that King Parikit is drawing ever closer to his death, occasioned by a young brahmin's curse. This story was recounted in *The Sages of Naimisharanya*, the first of our series.

Accepting the curse, Parikit made his way to the Ganges bank to fast and meditate until his death arrived. Thousands of sages assembled there, hearing of the curse, and among them was Shukadeva Goswami, deemed the best among them. He thus began to instruct Parikit, who started by asking the all-important question, "What is the duty of one about to die?"

This precipitated the recitation of *Srimad Bhagavatam*, whose purpose is to take us from spiritual ignorance to the highest point of pure love for God, Krishna. Before we meet Parikit and Shukadeva, we are introduced to Suta Goswami and a vast assembly of sages at Naimisharanya, a holy site in India. Their spokesperson, Shaunaka Rishi, is questioning Suta, who was present at the discussion between Shukadeva and Parikit. Suta thus relates that conversation, and the discussion between him and Shaunaka frames the entire *Bhagavatam*.

Coming now to canto eight, we are almost halfway through the *Bhagavatam*, which should mean that around three days have elapsed from when Shukadeva first began to speak. In fact, he only begins speaking in canto two, the first canto being entirely narrated by Suta. We have found it challenging to work out the *Bhagavatam's* timeline, assuming that the whole work, minus canto one, was spoken in the seven-day-and-night time frame. By our estimates, the time taken for reciting all the verses of cantos two to twelve in normal speech comes to considerably less than seven days and nights, but we think it likely that there would have been interludes of ecstatic contemplation during the recital. We conjecture that these would most likely have occurred during canto ten when Shukadeva speaks about the highly esoteric pastimes of Lord Krishna. With this in mind, we have tried our best to provide a timeline for the narration, but we realise this may not be accurate. Nevertheless, the timing is not so significant. Suffice it to say that the recitation was complete in seven days when Parikit at last departed for the spiritual world.

However, we have, as always, endeavoured to accurately present the *Bhagavatam's* philosophy and stories. These bestow wondrous benefits upon the reader, as the text repeatedly makes clear. Our single aim is to encourage our readers to delve more deeply into the pages of *Srimad Bhagavatam*, especially the translation by our esteemed spiritual teacher, Srila Prabhupada. Only by his grace have we been able to present this work, and we pray that he is pleased with our efforts. We also pray that he will show his grace to all our readers, enabling them to fully relish the transcendental bliss of this great spiritual treatise.

Hare Krishna
In service,
Krishna Dharma
Chintamani Dhama Dasi

ENCHANTING PASTIMES

1
The Universal Administrators

Even though only four days remained before Shringi's curse took effect, Parikit was ready to meet death fearlessly. Shukadeva's powerful instructions convinced him that he was an eternal spirit soul and would not die when his body was killed. He no longer felt anxious for his citizens' fate after his death, for he was confident that the assembled sages would disseminate Shukadeva's liberating teachings to them. He glanced up at the setting sun. This would be his third night of not sleeping, but he felt no fatigue. The sage's words were enlivening him more and more.

(1.1-3) Bowing his head, the king said, "My dear spiritual master, by your grace, I have heard extensively about Svayambhuva Manu's illustrious dynasty. I know there were other Manus, and I am curious to hear about their progeny. O learned brahmin, I have heard that Krishna also incarnated in the dynasties of those Manus, and I am eager to hear about them. Kindly recount all the Supreme Lord's pastimes in previous, current and future Manvantaras."

(1.4-6) Shukadeva said, "In this *kalpa*[1], there have already been six Manus, of whom Svayambhuva was the first. As you know, Svayambhuva had two daughters, Devahuti and Akuti. I have already told you about Devahuti's son, Lord Kapila.[2] Now, hear about Akuti's son, Yagya, another divine incarnation, who, like Kapila, delivered instructions on religion and philosophical knowledge."

(1.7-11) Shukadeva described how Svayambhuva retired to the forest with his wife, Satarupa, to perform austerities. "He stood on one leg for one hundred years and recited a prayer glorifying Vishnu. He prayed, 'This entire material world and everything in it is created by the Supreme Lord, who alone is not created. At the time of universal annihilation, only he remains awake, witnessing everything. No one knows him, but he knows everyone and everything. He pervades the entire material world as the Supersoul. One should only use that which he allots to each of us, and no one should infringe on another's property. Although no one can see him, do not think he does not see everything. Instead, always worship him, knowing him to be your constant companion and friend.

(1.12-13) "'The conditioned soul thinks in terms of dualities such as beginning, middle, and end, or mine and theirs. However, all such conceptions are absent in God. He has no beginning, middle or end, he does not belong to any group or nation, and there is no distinction between his soul and his body. The material universe emanating from him is also integral to him. He is the ultimate reality, completely incorporating everything. Since he pervades the material cosmos as the Supersoul, it is considered his body. He is called by many names and has unlimited energies. He creates the cosmos with his material energy but always remains aloof from it in his spiritual energy.

(1.14-16) "'We can only know him when we are on the spiritual platform and desire no result from our work. It is not possible to reach this position by artificially refraining from work. Great saints recommend that conditioned souls regulate their material activities according to the instructions of scripture. This will gradually purify them of material desires and enable them to work purely for Krishna's pleasure. Such work is spiritual and does not entangle one in worldly life. Just as Krishna is never entangled despite creating, maintaining, and annihilating the material cosmos, his devotees, whom he always guides, are also never ensnared. The Supreme Lord comes to this world and acts just like us, but he is not interested in enjoying the fruit of his work. He is completely independent in his happiness, and he comes to teach others how to connect with him and be happy. I request everyone to accept the method he teaches, known as bhakti yoga.'"

(1.17-18) Shukadeva continued, "Svayambhuva Manu was in a deep trance as he recited this prayer, taken from the Upanishads. Seeing him and thinking he was asleep and therefore helpless, some hungry demoniac cannibals surrounded him, desiring to eat him. However, his adoptive son, Yagyapati,[3] appeared, accompanied by his sons, the Yamas and other gods, to kill those cannibals before they could harm him. After that, Yagyapati accepted the post of Indra and ruled the heavens."

Parikit said, "How did Yagyapati know Svayambhuva Manu was in danger?"

"He is the Supreme Soul in everyone's heart."

(1.19-30) Shukadeva then listed the three Manus after Svayambhuva, their fathers' names, their principal sons, the name of Indra, the other gods, and the seven celestial sages during their reigns. He told of Krishna's different incarnations in each reign, culminating in how Vishnu rescued Gajendra, the king of the elephants, from a crocodile.

(1.31-32) Parikit's curiosity was aroused, and he asked Shukadeva to speak about this incident in more detail. "Surely, I shall recite this wondrous tale. Among all the histories glorifying Krishna, this one bestows on the hearer great purity, glory, auspiciousness, and fortune."[4]

(1.33) Shukadeva began the story of Gajendra.

2
Gajendra's Dilemma

(2.1-19) Thunderous pounding reverberated through the idyllic mountainous region of Trikuta. The Siddhas, Charanas, Gandharvas and Apsaras who were sporting on the jewel-strewn lake shores flew up, startled by the sound. What demon could have penetrated their heavenly abode? They scanned all directions. Nearby, the great mountain rose up into the sky, surrounded by a vast ocean of milk. Surveying the land from behind the clouds, the celestials could see the mountain's three prominent peaks: one of iron, another of silver, and the third of gold. There were no Asura hordes visible on any of them. Still, the pounding continued. Had the Rakshasas somehow breached the gods' defences? Their eyes scoured the landscape. Everything seemed peaceful enough. There were orchards of brightly blossoming trees, bushes, creepers and countless varieties of flowers blowing in the breeze, but no Asuras. Waterfalls cascaded pleasingly down the sides of the mountain, and waves from the milk ocean lapped at its foot, throwing up great gleaming emeralds that lay on the glistening beach. No demons were in sight, and yet the thundering grew still louder.

(2.20-24) Then from their vantage point high in the sky, the celestials noticed mighty elephants, tigers, lions, rhinoceroses, serpents and terrible six-legged *sharabhas* bolting in fear from the Ritumat Gardens, Varuna's exquisite pleasure grounds. Concealing themselves behind clouds, they cautiously drew closer to see if the Asuras were hidden behind the exotic plants and trees that decorated that region. None were visible. Suddenly a colossal elephant broke through the foliage. The celestials gasped in wonder. The beast broke down huge trees as it lumbered toward a great lake filled with golden lotuses. The earth and sky seemed to shake with its every step. Though larger animals fled in fear of him, smaller ones like rabbits, foxes and monkeys seemed reassured by his presence. The celestials looked at each other in confusion. Was this a demon in disguise? Should they alert Indra? As they stared in amazement at the behemoth, they noticed behind it a train of she-elephants and their calves.

"This seems more like a family outing than a raid," one Gandharva remarked. At that moment, Varuna arrived and confirmed they had nothing to fear. "This is Gajendra, king of the elephants."

They smiled in relief. Intrigued, they flew closer to examine the extraordinary creature that had startled them.

Gajendra was perspiring, liquor exuded from his temples, and his eyes rolled from intoxication. Bees hovered around him, drinking his perspiration as if it was nectar. He could smell the fragrance of lotuses carried on the breeze from a distance. Surrounded by his wives and children, all afflicted by thirst, he soon arrived at the lake shore.

(2.25-26) The elephant king plunged into the vast lake sending great waves far out into its waters. He languished in the cool waters until he was relieved of his fatigue, leisurely drinking the aromatic waters to satiate his thirst. Many of the she-elephants followed him into the water, but some stayed with the smaller calves that were too nervous about venturing in. Out of love for them, Gajendra went close to the shore and, with his trunk, sprayed them with water. As his children squealed with pleasure, he trumpeted in happiness. The she-elephants entered the water, leaving the children to play with their doting father. Their thirst slaked, the calves lay contentedly by the lakeside and dozed. Gajendra turned and waded deeper into the waters. Sporting with his wives, he splashed and pushed them playfully while trumpeting exuberantly.

(2.27-30) Gajendra's heavy steps shook the lakebed and disturbed a fierce crocodile dwelling there. Becoming enraged, the monstrous aquatic swam unseen to the source of the disturbance. Opening his mouth wide, he closed his dagger-like teeth over Gajendra's leathery leg. Gajendra screamed in pain as his blood reddened the waters. He tried frantically to pull his leg back. The waters churned, and the scaly tail of the gigantic crocodile thrashed about. His wives and children trumpeted in fear. Some she elephants tried to pull Gajendra back with their trunks, but they could not resist the crocodile's strength. As their mighty husband slipped deeper into the lake, they lost their hold on him and wailed loudly.

Overcoming his initial shock, Gajendra struggled with all his might to reach the shore. Hearing the commotion, the celestials gathered above and watched as the two titans hauled one another in and out of the water. The astonishing struggle continued for a very long time. Neither could gain ascendence over the other, but gradually Gajendra was weakening. He had lost much blood and struggled to move in the lake's depths. He found it increasingly difficult to resist the crocodile, fighting within its own habitat.

(2.31-33) Finding himself pulled deeper into the water, Gajendra realised he was helpless and unable to protect himself from this peril. Fear overwhelmed him. Who could save him? Looking back at his relatives, he saw them weeping helplessly on the riverbank. It was surely his destined time to die. None of the other elephants could help him escape his karma.[5] There was only one person who could override destiny, the all-powerful Lord Vishnu. He could protect anyone from the reactions of their past sins. Very few understood his power and influence. Gajendra felt hope. It was fortunate that in his hour of need, when the powerful serpent of time was about to swallow him, he remembered the Lord. As he meditated on Vishnu, a deep sense of peace swept over him. Surely that Supreme Person, who is everyone's shelter, would give him protection if he surrendered to him.

3
Gajendra Liberated

Parikit had a doubt. "Gajendra was an elephant. How did he know that he would be saved by surrendering to Krishna?"

(3.1) Shukadeva said, "In his previous life, Gajendra was the great devotee, King Indradyumna. Therefore, by Krishna's grace, he received the intelligence to fix his mind on the Lord and recite a mantra he knew in his life as Indradyumna. Listen to what happened next."

***

(3.2-3) Feeling helpless, Gajendra prayed. "I meditate on the Supreme Lord, the original person from whom everything has come and on whom it all depends. He is worshipped even by the great deities Brahma and Shiva. Only because he accompanies us, individual souls, as the Supersoul, do our material bodies function. However, although the entire material cosmos comes from and depends on him, he is different and independent.

(3.4-6) "The Lord expands his energy to create and destroy the material universes. He is everything and, at the same time, transcendental to everything. I now seek his protection. He alone continues to exist after the cosmic annihilation. However, no one perceives him, just as the audience does not recognise an actor on stage.

(3.7-9) "Virtuous sages desire to attain the shelter of his lotus-like feet, as do I. He has no material birth, form, name, or qualities. Nevertheless, he appears in the material world in a human-like form through his spiritual energy. He is supremely powerful, and in all his incarnations, he acts wonderfully.

(3.10-12) "I offer him my respects, for although he cannot be detected by any material method, he sees all. He enables those who serve him in transcendental love to realise him and thus experience the greatest happiness. I offer my obeisance to his transcendental incarnations, his form as the material universe, and his manifestation as the impersonal Brahman effulgence."

The crocodile pulled Gajendra still deeper into the lake. The elephant could barely keep his trunk above the water. He could not last much longer. He trembled in fear. Would the Lord help him? He prayed even more fervently.

(3.13-16) "O Supreme Lord, I offer you my obeisance. You are the Supersoul, the supreme controller and witness of everything. My body and everything else in this world are yours. Please remove my doubts. Please show me how this universe is your shadow, and only appears to have substance because of you. My Lord, cause of all causes, including the scriptures and the saintly teachers, I bow to you. You shelter your devotees, freeing us from our material entanglement. Just as fire is present in *arani* wood[6], even when not manifest, you are present everywhere, even though unseen. Thus, you know everything. Being independent, you can reveal yourself in the minds of your pure devotees.

(3.17) "Even though I am a dumb animal, I surrender to you. Since you are free to do as you wish, please release me from this dangerous situation. I know that being supremely merciful, you reside in my heart and are always trying to rescue me from the repetition of birth and death, but I have foolishly rejected your help until now. Nevertheless, I know you never give up on us out of anger. Therefore, I offer you, who perfectly knows everything, my respect."

(3.18) Tears welled in Gajendra's eyes. Why had he turned away from the Lord for so long? He lamented, "The pure-hearted do not wait for calamities to think of you. They never forget you. Those like me who are overly attached to material enjoyment with family and friends, thinking ourselves very powerful, find it difficult to attain you. Only by your mercy am I now becoming free of these false attachments. Therefore, I offer you my respectful obeisance."

Still, the crocodile dragged Gajendra farther into the lake. Soon only his head and tusks were visible. Gajendra berated himself. He had been so proud of his strength and used his time to enjoy unlimited sexual pleasure with his many wives. Now, look at his condition. What was the value of such a materialistic life, which must end in suffering?

(3.19) Straining to keep his head above the waters with the crocodile's jaws still clamped around his leg, Gajendra trumpeted his prayer up to the skies, "O unlimitedly merciful Lord, you are famous for fulfilling the desires of even those who worship you for material happiness and liberation. Indeed, out of your causeless mercy, you even sometimes give such worshippers a place in your abode. Please deliver me both from this present danger and material life."

(3.20-21) Again and again, he repented. "If I were a true devotee, I would not ask you for anything because my mind would be merged in transcendental happiness by hearing, chanting and remembering you. Alas, my Lord, I am a fallen soul. I am frightened, and I beg you to please protect me."

The crocodile pulled him into deeper water, but still, the Lord did not appear. Only Gajendra's eyes and trunk remained above the surface.

(3.22-24) By Krishna's grace, prayers he knew in his previous life continued to come to his mind. "My Lord, you have two types of expansions: minor and major. Minor expansions include all conditioned souls, from Lord Brahma and the personified Vedic rituals down to the lowest of creatures.[7] The major expansions are your Vishnu forms and your empowered incarnations.[8] We conditioned souls are like sparks of a fire or the sun's rays. The different layers of material covering, like the mind, intelligence, senses, and the modes of nature, are also your minor expansions. You are the source of everything yet are simultaneously aloof. When all else is negated, you alone remain. All glory to you, the unlimited Supreme Person."

(3.25) As his head submerged, he heard the Supersoul in his heart. "Do you desire to be rescued so you can continue your life as the king of elephants?"[9]

A sense of detachment had awoken in Gajendra's heart. "No, my Lord. I no longer wish to live in this elephant's body, even if you release me from the crocodile's jaws."

"Then what do you want?"

"I desire that freedom which cannot be destroyed by time;[10] freedom from ignorance."

(3.26) Gajendra prayed with all his heart. "Lord! Supreme Person! You create the universe, and yet you are transcendental to it. You are unborn, always supreme, and you know everything. I offer you my obeisance and beg you to release me from material existence."

(3.27-28) Tears rolled down Gajendra's face. "What hope is there for me to attain you? I am just an animal. Great devotees achieve freedom from birth and death by performing bhakti yoga, but I cannot do so.[11] You only protect those who have fully surrendered to you. Since I have never practised controlling my senses, I am not eligible to receive your mercy without which no one can appreciate your greatness or sweetness."

Deep in Gajendra's heart, a small voice spoke to him: "It is not too late to surrender."

(3.29) Gajendra called out, "I surrender to you, my Lord, by whose energy I have forgotten my real spiritual identity and think I am an elephant."[12]

(3.30) In the heavens, the gods observed everything, but none moved to help Gajendra. One Gandharva said, "Should we assist him?"

"Why should we?" retorted Indra. "Gajendra has neither glorified us nor prayed to us. If anything, he belittled us by calling us minor expansions. Let the Supreme Lord in whom he has so much faith come and rescue him."

The Gandharva said, "The Lord does not get involved in the petty troubles of this world. He has appointed you gods to deal with that, to protect the righteous."

"The elephant should have considered that before scorning our authority. It seems he will now die."[13]

(3.31) Just then, they saw an effulgent four-armed form riding on the back of a great eagle descending from above and moving swiftly toward Gajendra. With him were Brahma on his swan carrier and Shiva on his bull. They were reciting prayers glorifying Vishnu.

Indra and the other gods looked on in surprise.

"That is Lord Vishnu on Garuda's back," said Chandra. "It seems he wishes to show his mercy to this elephant. See how quickly he hurries to him carrying his disc and other weapons."

Worried that Vishnu would disapprove of their supercilious attitude toward Gajendra, they all quickly called for their mounts and hurried to accompany him.

(3.32) Gajendra, screaming in pain, was being forcefully pulled under the water. Seeing Lord Vishnu wielding his disc, riding toward him on Garuda's back, he used his last strength to pluck a lotus flower with his trunk. He offered it up to Vishnu with these words, "O my Lord, Narayana, master of the universe, O Supreme Person, please accept my obeisance."

(3.33) Anxious that Garuda would not reach the distressed elephant in time to save him, Lord Narayana leapt from his carrier's back and dashed toward him. He seized Gajendra and pulled him and the crocodile onto the shore. As the gods watched in astonishment, he severed the crocodile's head from his body and saved Gajendra.

4
Gajendra's Past Life

(4.1) Shukadeva said, "When the Supreme Lord rescued Gajendra, all the gods, sages and Gandharvas, headed by Brahma and Shiva, praised him and showered flowers on them both. Musicians in the heavens beat kettledrums while the Gandharvas sang and danced. The sages from Charanaloka and Siddhaloka recited eloquent prayers glorifying the Lord."

Shukadeva paused and looked at Parikit as if to say that was the end of the history of Gajendra's deliverance. Parikit was intrigued to know more. "The crocodile was highly blessed to be killed by Vishnu. How did he achieve such good fortune?"

(4.3-5) "In his previous life, he was King Huhu, the Gandharva leader," replied Shukadeva. "Once, while playing in a lake with women, he grabbed Sage Devala by his foot and pulled him under. Devala became angry and cursed him to become a crocodile. However, after Huhu pacified him, he blessed him that Vishnu would personally free him from the curse when he attacked Gajendra.[14] When he was released from the crocodile body, Huhu remembered this incident and offered the Lord many prayers of glorification. Then, freed of all sinful reactions by Krishna's causeless mercy, he circumambulated the Lord, offered his obeisance, and in the presence of all the gods headed by Brahma, returned to Gandharvaloka."

"What happened to Gajendra after his rescue?" asked Parikit.

(4.6) "He was immediately freed from the elephant's body and all material ignorance. Touched by the Supreme Lord's hands, he attained the liberation known as *sarupya-mukti*; in other words, he achieved a body just like the Lord's with four hands and wearing yellow garments."

"Please tell me more about his previous life," said Parikit.

(4.7-10) "As the great devotee King Indradyumna, he ruled Pandya, a country in Southern India. At the appropriate age, King Indradyumna retired from family life and went to an ashrama in the Malaya Hills. He lived like a hermit with matted locks, always engaged in asceticism. Once, observing a vow of silence, he became absorbed in worshipping the Lord while in a trance of ecstatic love. At that time, the sage Agastya happened to arrive at his ashram along with his many disciples. Indradyumna, unaware of his presence, failed to greet or offer him any hospitality. Infuriated, Agastya uttered the following curse. 'This King Indradyumna has no manners. He is degraded and unintelligent; otherwise, how could he so brazenly insult a brahmin? Therefore, I curse him to receive an ignorant body befitting his mentality. Let him become an elephant.'

(4.11-13) "As soon as he spoke these words, Indradyumna's breathing became difficult. He opened his eyes to see Agastya and his disciples marching away. Grasping his throat, he fell to the ground. What was happening to him? One of Agastya's disciple's felt sorry to see his distress and bewilderment. He hung back and told the dying king what had happened. Indradyumna felt no anger toward Agastya for his harsh treatment. He welcomed the curse, accepting it as Krishna's will. Due to his devotional service as Indradyumna, he remembered how to worship and offer prayers to Vishnu even when in an elephant's body. Consequently, the Lord delivered him simultaneously from the crocodile's clutches and material existence, which resembles a crocodile. He was awarded a form like the Lord's. Then while Gandharvas, Siddhas and other gods sang hymns glorifying the Lord, Narayana seated Gajendra on the back of Garuda with him, and together they returned to his eternal spiritual abode."

(4.14-15) Shukadeva drew a deep breath. "Thus ends the history of how Krishna wonderfully rescued Gajendra, the elephant king. My dear Parikit, best among the Kurus, just by hearing this history, anyone can be promoted to the higher planets, become reputed as a great saintly devotee, be protected from the bad qualities of Kali Yuga and never experience nightmares. If due to committing sinful activities you experience a bad dream, you should recite this history as soon as you wake up to become free of any lingering mental disturbance."

Parikit said, "Not everyone knows this story."

"That's true," replied Shukadeva. "However, *vaishyas*, *kshatriyas* and brahmins who have studied under a bona fide spiritual master will probably know it. Certainly, Vaishnavas will."

Parikit nodded. "May I ask if Lord Narayana said anything to Gajendra after rescuing him?"

(4.16-25) Shukadeva beamed with pleasure on hearing the question. "Yes. Lord Narayana was so pleased with Gajendra that he blessed him in the presence of all the celestials. The Lord said, 'To any pious souls who rise early and meditate on my eternal form, my energies, my expansions and associates, on this pastime with you, and the prayers you have offered me, I will grant an eternal residence in the spiritual world at the end of their lives.'

(4.26) "Then the Lord blew his conch, the Panchajanya, whose transcendental sound is most pleasing to the celestials, and departed on the back of Garuda."

***

Shaunaka and the sages were struck with wonder. They were amazed that a dumb elephant attained Vaikuntha, a goal which even great mystics found difficult to achieve.

Shaunaka said, "Has anyone noticed the similarity between this history and that of Parikit?"

An elderly ascetic said, "Both Indradyumna and Parikit were cursed for an unwitting offence."

"Exactly," said Shaunaka. "Furthermore, neither became angry nor retaliated. Is that not remarkable?"

"Devotees are always tolerant," Suta replied. "We also saw this with Chitraketu, who did not become angry when unfairly cursed by Mother Parvati."

"How is this possible?" asked Shaunaka. "Anger is such a powerful emotion."

Many sages muttered in agreement. One said, "Even the mother of the universe, Parvati, fell victim to anger."

"True," agreed another sage. "We ascetics who have controlled our eating, mating and sleeping are also susceptible to anger."

Turning to Suta, he asked, "What is the devotees' special secret, dear Suta? How is it they can forgive even those who wrong them?"

Suta said, "This prayer may shed light on their excellent character. 'My dear Lord, one who earnestly waits for you to bestow your causeless mercy upon him, all the while patiently suffering the reactions of his past misdeeds and offering you all respects with his heart, words and body, is surely eligible for liberation for it has become his rightful claim.'"[15]

A young brahmin said, "I thought Krishna protects his surrendered devotees from the reactions of their past misdeeds.[16] So what is the question of them patiently suffering such reactions?

"Krishna certainly protects his surrendered devotee from his past sinful reactions," said Suta. "However, until we are established in our eternal relationship with Krishna, there will be a slight inclination to enjoy false material happiness. Krishna rectifies this tendency by giving some small punishments. These may resemble sinful reactions, but it is the Lord's special mercy for inducing his devotee to make further spiritual advancement."[17]

The sages loudly cheered, and Shaunaka asked Suta to continue narrating Shukadeva's instructions to Parikit.

5
The Gods Cursed

(5.1-3) Shukadeva said, "My dear king, the history of Gajendra's liberation is most auspicious. Hearing such divine pastimes can free one from all sinful reactions. Now please listen as I narrate the history of Raivata, who became the fifth Manu after his brother Tamasa.[18]

(5.4-5) "During his term as Manu, there was a sage called Shubhra whose wife was Vikuntha.[19] The Supreme Lord, Vaikuntha, and his plenary expansions took birth as their sons. Vaikuntha's brothers became the gods. To please his wife, the goddess of fortune, Vaikuntha manifested another Vaikuntha planet which is worshipped in the same way as the Lord's other spiritual planets."

"Where is this planet?"

"It is within this universe, just above the Lokaloka mountain."[20]

"How can a spiritual planet be within the material universe?"

(5.6) "Everything is possible for Krishna," said Shukadeva. "If you could count the atoms in this one universe, maybe you could count his transcendental qualities. They are without limit. No one can understand Krishna's spiritual opulence."

Parikit's face reddened. "Yes, of course, you are right. Please forgive my impudence. Kindly continue telling me about the Manus."

(5.7-10) Shukadeva smiled at the king's humility and continued to describe the details of the sixth Manu's reign.[21] "During the time of Chakshusha Manu, the Lord incarnated as Ajita, the son of Vairaja and Devasambhuti. In that incarnation, Krishna became a tortoise and supported Mandara Mountain. During this episode, nectar was produced by churning the milk ocean and later distributed to the gods."

(5.11-12) Parikit opened his eyes wide in wonder. "This sounds like a fascinating history. I am keen to know more. Why did Krishna incarnate as a tortoise to hold up Mount Mandara? How did he churn the milk ocean? How did the gods receive the nectar? Was anything else produced during the churning? Please tell me everything."

Shukadeva said, "Why do you want so much detail?"

(5.13) Tears fell from Parikit's eyes. "My heart is always disturbed by the sufferings of material existence. The only remedy which alleviates my pain is hearing descriptions of Krishna's pastimes."

(5.14) Shukadeva looked with affection at the king. "It is your great good fortune that you have developed a strong attraction for hearing about Krishna. This will ensure your eternal welfare. Now, please listen as I describe the history of Lord Kurma, the divine tortoise."

***

(5.15-16) With his head held high, Indra rode down the wide roads of Amaravati on the back of his great elephant, Airavata. He was flanked by other prominent gods and followed by his vast army. The celestials lined the roads cheering the procession with chants of "Long live King Indra!" Brahmins chanted auspicious mantras of welcome. Gandharvas sang and played musical instruments. Beautiful Apsaras danced and scattered fragrant flower petals on the victorious gods. Many citizens ran forward to garland the returning heroes. The warriors shone brilliantly in their jewelled armours. Decked with an abundance of fragrant flower garlands, they smiled and waved to the jubilant crowd.

Durvasa and his thousand disciples happened to be visiting the heavens at this time. Caught up in the fervour of the reception, Durvasa removed from his neck a celestial garland he had earlier received from Vishnu. Pushing through the crowd, he approached Indra, calling, "Indra, king of heaven, I commend you!"

With these words, the sage held up his divine garland to offer to Indra. Intoxicated with his victory, Indra leaned over and plucked the garland from the sage's hands without acknowledging him. Durvasa scowled. He had expected Indra to descend from his elephant, offer his respects, and allow Durvasa to garland him personally. The sage looked around. People everywhere were calling out their congratulations.

"All glory to Indra, mighty king of the gods!"

Durvasa stepped back. Never mind, it was understandable that Indra should be overcome with pride, given the circumstances. Then, to the sage's horror, Indra, already weighted with many garlands, tossed Durvasa's garland onto Airavata's head. As

Durvasa looked on, the startled elephant, disliking the intense fragrance of the garland, tossed it into the air. As if in slow motion, the garland span to the ground and was crushed beneath the feet of the marching beast.

Durvasa's neck and face turned a bright scarlet. His eyebrows furrowed, and his eyes became like red hot coals. Unheedful of the sage's anger, Indra rode past, waving happily to the adoring crowds.

"Indra! You fool!" bellowed Durvasa. His voice resounded like thunder, rising above the chatter of the crowds. Everyone ceased their revelry and turned to see who had disrupted the victory parade. Durvasa's eyes seemed to emit fire as he stood with legs planted firmly apart, his right arm stretched out, pointing angrily up at Indra.

"Proud of your opulence, you have dared to disregard my gift! I curse you and the three planetary systems you govern to become bereft of all fortune. As you have cast down my garland, so shall you be cast down."

Indra leapt from his elephant, his face a mask of horror. Upsetting the irascible Durvasa was a terrible blunder. He fell to his knees and begged the sage for forgiveness, but the implacable Durvasa stormed off angrily, followed by his many disciples. All of them stared straight ahead and ignored all pleas for clemency.

Immediately Indra and the other gods felt their power and influence desert them. Their bodily lustre diminished, and their minds became despondent.

"Alas!" cried Indra. "What have I done? Now we face destruction. When they hear of this curse, the Asuras will surely attack."

As Indra had feared, the Asura chief Bali had received word of Durvasa's curse. He spoke at once to his ministers. "Hear me, Asura generals; our time has come. The gods are now weak. Let us immediately sally forth and crush them."

The cheering Asuras swarmed up from the lower planets and rushed upon Amaravati. "Slay them! Chop them up. Spare none!" they cried as they spurred on their mounts and drove their great golden chariots. They fell upon the gods with tremendous roars, discharging countless serpent-like weapons. Although the gods valiantly fended off the attack, they were soon overcome. Many were slain, and the decimated celestial army fled.

(5.17-18) Indra, Varuna and a few other surviving gods realised they were in grave peril. The Asuras would want to finish the job. Consulting together, they could think of no solution other than to seek Lord Brahma's shelter.

Wounded, tired and dishevelled, they fled to Brahma's abode, where they fell before the great deity in obeisance.

"My dear gods," said Brahma. "What has happened to you?"

(5.19-20) On hearing everything and understanding the danger facing both the gods and the three planetary systems, Brahma began to meditate on Vishnu. When he finished, he felt enlivened and he reassured the gods.

(5.21) "Ultimately, all beings have come from the Supreme Person. It may seem that some species came from the progenitors or me, but I am merely the incarnation of the Lord's mode of passion, and the progenitors come from me. So he is the origin of all beings. Therefore, best we seek Lord Vishnu's guidance, which benefits everyone.

(5.22) "After all, he is equal to both you and the Asuras. He neither hates nor favours anyone, nor is he inclined to kill or protect anyone."

The gods looked concerned. They depended upon his intervention. Indra said, "Why do we see so much killing if the Lord does not kill? Does he not especially kill the Asuras to protect the pious?"[22]

"The Lord does not personally kill. He acts through his energies. Utilising the mode of passion he creates, through ignorance he destroys, and by goodness he protects."

The gods glanced at one another. How were they to be saved?

(5.23) Brahma smiled. "Since you require the Lord's protection, you need to act in goodness which means following his guidance. The Lord is inclined toward you gods. Therefore, if you accept his advice, he will surely bestow good fortune on you."

(5.24) Brahma mounted his swan carrier, and followed by the gods, he swiftly travelled to the island of Svetadvipa, situated in the Milk Ocean, to confer with Lord Vishnu."

(5.25) Arriving at Svetadvipa, some of the gods' retinue looked around, expecting to see Vishnu, but he was nowhere visible. When Brahma started offering him eloquent prayers, one celestial whispered to the Ashvini Kumara brothers, "Who is he talking to?"

"Lord Vishnu," came the reply.

"I can't see Vishnu. Can you?"

The Ashvini god shook his head.

"Can Brahma see him, do you think?"

"Probably not. Vishnu is only perceived when he so desires."[23]

"If he cannot see him, how can he speak to him?"

The Ashvini frowned at the doubting celestial. "He does not have to see the Lord. Vedic evidence is sufficient to know he is present."

The lesser celestial thanked the Ashvini with folded palms. "Forgive my doubts."

(5.26-28) Brahma prayed loudly so all the gods could hear and join in his appeal. He said, "I offer my obeisance to Lord Vishnu, the unchanging, unlimited supreme truth, the origin of everything. You are in everyone's heart and every atom. Since you are not material, we can neither properly understand nor describe you, but we accept you as the Supreme, venerable Lord of all. You know everything, including each living being, their desires and thoughts. You control everyone and everything. Since you do not have a material body, you are not affected by karmic reactions, nor are you subject to ignorance. Indeed, you can enlighten everyone. I seek your shelter, for you are the Supreme Lord who incarnates with six excellences[24] in Satya, Treta and Dvapara Yugas. You are sometimes compared to the axle of the fast-moving wheel of a chariot, and our material bodies are compared to the chariot. Our senses, life airs, the modes of nature, the mind and the elements make up the different parts of the chariot wheel."

(5.29-30) Brahma turned to the gods. "Join me in offering our obeisance to Lord Vishnu, who is situated in pure goodness, untouched by the ignorance of the material world. He is always near us, but those of us subject to the ignorance of material consciousness cannot see him. Only the perfect yogis who are undisturbed by material dualities can see him. My dear gods, without surrendering to Lord Vishnu, one will remain bewildered and thus become frustrated in life. Only by his grace can anyone understand how to attain success. Without discrimination, he will enlighten anyone who seeks his shelter.

(5.31) "Even we gods in the mode of goodness fail to understand the Lord though he is present externally as time and internally as the Supersoul.[25] What can be expected of the demoniac atheists governed by ignorance and passion? They can never understand him. Since we can only know anything about him by his grace, let us offer him our respectful obeisance.[26]

The gods looked despondent. If even the great Brahma knew nothing about Vishnu, what hope was there for them?

(5.32) Brahma understood their worry. He said, "I know something about the Lord's manifestation in the material world. For example, I know that the material universe, along with the four kinds of living beings inhabiting it, is manifested by his unlimited opulence and that the entire material universe rests upon his lotus feet. Therefore, I understand the importance of pleasing him."

The gods looked confused. One of them voiced their common doubt. "There are so many species of life in the universe. Why do you say just four kinds?"

Another added, "I have this doubt and another one too. I thought the material universe rested on the stalk of the lotus flower growing from Garbhodakasayi Vishnu's abdomen. Why did you say it rests on his lotus feet?"

Brahma said, "Firstly, all the different species of life can be categorised into four types: those born from embryos, from eggs, from perspiration,[27] and from seeds. Regarding your second question, you are thinking of what happens within each universal egg. However, all the universes float in the *mahat-tattva*, which rests on the Lord's lotus feet.[28]

"What else do you know?" asked one of the attentive gods.

(5.33) "The entire world and all its inhabitants come from and depend on water. Some say this life-giving water is Krishna's semen, and others say it is his perspiration.[29] Either way, this should give us a clue as to the importance of pleasing him."

Soma, the moon god, said. "I thought all beings, including the gods, depended on me for their strength and longevity."

(5.34) Brahma said, "Dear Soma, your rays are essential to produce nutritious food grains necessary for everyone, including the gods, to live a long and healthy life. However, you should know that you receive your potency from the Lord's mind. He is the source of all opulence, even yours. Therefore, we must please him."

(5.35-36) Brahma addressed all the gods. "All your powers depend on the Lord. Agni's fire is the Lord's mouth by which he receives sacrificial oblations. As the fire of digestion in everyone's stomach. it is the Lord's opulence. Surya is famous for opening the path of liberation for yogis, for being the embodiment of Vedic knowledge,[30] and the source of life and death. This is also due to Krishna's empowerment, and Surya is of course famous as the Lord's eye."

(5.37) Brahma turned to Vayu. "The vital force of all beings, both moving and non-moving, depends on you. Indeed, to live, we all need the air you supply. However, the air originally comes from Vishnu. Therefore, you, too, need to please him."

(5.38) He swept his arm about, encompassing all the celestials. "You all come from and depend on Vishnu. You gods of the directions are generated from his ears. You who control the living entities' eyes, ears, nostrils, rectum and genitals come from his heart. You gods controlling the secondary life airs[31] within the body, receive empowerment from Vishnu's transcendental body."

(5.39) Brahma pointed to Indra. "Your strength also comes from Vishnu. All the gods were generated by the Lord's mercy, except for Shiva and me."

Indra asked, "Where do you come from?"

"Shiva was generated by Vishnu's anger and I from his intelligence. Even the Vedic mantras are generated from the Lord's pores, and the saintly universal progenitors come from his genitals. We all depend entirely on the Lord, and therefore we all must please him."

Surya said, "Is this true of all celestials or just us principal gods?"

(5.40) "Everyone from major to minor gods come from Vishnu. The goddess of fortune comes from his chest, the inhabitants of Pitriloka from his shadow, religion from his chest and irreligion from his back. The heavenly planets were generated from the crown of his head and the Apsaras from his sense of enjoyment. Everyone depends on the Lord's pleasure to function."

Chandra said, "I see how we celestials need to be empowered by Vishnu, but how is that the case with normal mortals?"

(5.41) "Everyone gets their ability from Krishna," replied Brahma. "For example, both the brahmins and the Vedas come from the Lord's mouth; the *kshatriyas,* along with their strength, come from his arms; the *vaishyas* and their agricultural and entrepreneurial expertise, comes from his thighs; and the *shudras,* along with their different inclinations to serve come from his feet. Therefore, to succeed in any field of activity, one must please the Lord."

Surya looked thoughtful. "How about sinful people? Do they also get their inclinations from Vishnu?

(5.42) "Yes. Everything, whether good, bad, or neutral, comes from Vishnu. For example, greed is generated from his lower lip, affection from his upper lip, bodily lustre from his nose, kindness toward animals comes from his touch,[32] Yamaraja, the lord of death, comes from his eyebrows, and eternal time from his eyelashes.

(5.43) "Suffice it to say that the Lord's creative energy produces this material world; that is why it is inconceivable. Not only is the working of the entire universe baffling, but even our bodies' function is bewildering. We should stop trying to control the material world, but rather determine to leave it."

One of the Ashvini Kumara brothers said, "Why should we reject the Lord's wondrous creation?"

"Because both the great sages and Krishna himself advise us to do so," said Brahma.

(5.44) Brahma surveyed the group of bedraggled gods kneeling before him. "Even if we cannot see him, even if he does not speak to us, we must offer him our obeisance."

Indra said, "What does he want from us?"

Brahma smiled. "He is completely self-satisfied. He is not attached to anything in this world. Even when he comes here to perform pastimes, he wants nothing for himself. However, it is good for us to surrender to him."

Pleased with Brahma, Vishnu spoke from within his heart. "My dear Brahma, you may ask of me any boon."[33]

Brahma became very still; his whole countenance shone with a brilliant effulgence. The other gods looked at each other. They could tell he was having a profoundly mystical experience. They became quiet, eager to hear anything Brahma might say.

(5.45-46) Brahma spoke in a reverential tone. "Lord, we are your surrendered devotees. Kindly show us your eternal form."

"Which of my forms do you wish to realise: impersonal or personal?"

"Please show us your personal feature, Lord, so that we can see your smiling, lotus-like face. That original form is the source of your innumerable incarnations[34], which appear in every age to perform wonderful activities impossible for anyone else.

(5.47-49) "Dear Lord, please do not let your devotees be baffled like the hard-working materialists. Unlike them, we devotees have dedicated our lives to your service. They think that work is the cause of success, but sometimes it simply results in frustration. We devotees know that by your grace, all things are possible. You are so affectionate to anyone who serves you that you offer them the greatest result, even for a little service rendered. As pouring water on a tree's root benefits the entire tree, satisfying you is sufficient to benefit all beings. Conversely, without pleasing you, even doing one's prescribed duties perfectly is useless."[35]

(5.50) Brahma bowed his head. "My Lord, since you are unlimited, we cannot fully understand you. Therefore, I do not know whether you will fulfil our desires, but we offer you our obeisance in all circumstances.[36]

The Lord spoke to Brahma from within his heart. "Or possibly you offer respect because you think I am merciful and will certainly fulfil your desires."

Brahma bowed his four heads. "My Lord, I know that out of your mercy, you sometimes do and sometimes do not fulfil your devotees' material desires, depending on what is best for their spiritual advancement."

"Why pray to me if you think I may not fulfil your desire?"[37]

Brahma's face broke into a child-like smile. "I know that those in the mode of goodness are meant to be prominent in this current era, and that you manage the mode of goodness. Therefore, I think there is a good chance you will support the gods who are in goodness."[38]

6
The Truce

(6.1-2) A dazzling light blinded the gods. They could not see the sky or anything in any direction. They could not even see themselves.

Surya called out, "Where is this light coming from?"

"We thought it was you," another god replied.

"This is thousands of times more powerful than my rays."

Brahma calmed the startled gods. "This is Lord Kshirodakashayi Vishnu's bodily radiance. Pleased by our prayers, he is appearing before us."[39]

"How do you know?" called out Indra. "I can't see him. This light has completely blinded me."

Other gods called out, "Same with me!"

(6.3-7) "Well, I can see him." said Brahma.

"So can I," said Shiva.

Brahma and Shiva took turns describing the vision before them for the benefit of the other gods.

"His beauty is without blemish, and his complexion is blackish like a *marakata* gem," said Brahma.

Shiva added, "His eyes are a reddish hue like the whorl of a lotus flower, and his garments are yellow like molten gold."

Brahma said, "His entire body is gorgeously decorated, and a charming smile and attractive eyebrows enhance his beauty."

"Please describe the Lord's decorations," said one of the gods.

Shiva said, "His head is crowned with a bejewelled helmet, his cheeks are adorned with earrings, and he wears a belt on his waist."

Brahma added, "He has bangles on his arms, a necklace on his chest, and ankle bells on his legs."

Shiva said, "He is bedecked with flower garlands, and his neck is decorated with the Kaustubha gem. Look! He has the goddess of fortune on his chest."

"Yes, yes, I see!" said Brahma. "And see how his personified weapons like the *chakra* worship him."[40]

As he said this, the other gods' eyes became accustomed to the glare, and they, too, could see Vishnu. All the gods, including Brahma and Shiva, fell to the ground to offer their prostrated obeisance.

(6.8) Rising to his knees, Brahma spoke in a love-choked voice. "Dear Lord, you are never born but always appear in your wondrous incarnations. You exist eternally in your transcendental form, the source of a boundless ocean of eternal spiritual bliss."

Suddenly a spectacular vision manifested before him.

(6.9) Gasping in surprise, Brahma said, "I...I can see the entire universe, including myself and all the other gods in your body. How amazing! You are certainly superior to all. Since everything is ultimately under your direction, those who desire their good fortune must worship you."

Vishnu smiled. "All you gods are also important; many people like to worship you."[41]

(6.10-11) Brahma realised Vishnu was testing him. "My Lord, only you are fully independent; we all receive strength from you. As a clay pot comes from, rests on, and finally returns to the earth, this entire universe arises from you, is supported by you, and in the end returns to you. You use your energies to create the cosmos, and then you enter it and remain here. Nevertheless, you are never affected by the material qualities."

"How do you know that?" asked Vishnu.

"Those advanced in spiritual consciousness, fully knowledgeable of revealed scriptures, can see these truths with clear minds unaffected by the modes of nature."

"Since material qualities do not touch me, how do they see me?" asked Vishnu.[42]

(6.12) "Just as by your decree we can get fire by rubbing wood, or milk from a cow, or food grains from the land, or earn our livelihood by work, similarly humans can realise you by executing the practices of bhakti yoga, like hearing about and glorifying you, thinking of you and worshipping you."

Vishnu nodded to show his approval of Brahma's answer.

(6.13) Feeling encouraged, Brahma said, "O Lord, just as elephants afflicted by a forest fire become happy on entering the Ganges River, we are in transcendental bliss on seeing you. We have hankered for this for a very long time, and today we feel we have achieved the goal of our lives.

(6.14) "My Lord, kindly accomplish what we have come here to ask for. Since you are the Supersoul within and without, you already know what we require."

Vishnu smiled. "Because of humility, you think you do not know how to accomplish your desires. Thus you are leaving the matter to my discretion. However, I know you are highly intelligent. Therefore, please tell me what you think is the solution to your problem, and I will accomplish it."[43]

(6.15) Brahma placed his palms together. "Since all of us are tiny sparks of you, we do not know what is best for us. Therefore, please instruct us how both the gods and the brahmins may benefit.

(6.16) Vishnu understood Brahma's heart. He wanted to know how the gods could regain sovereignty over the heavenly planets.[44]

(6.17-19) Vishnu remained silent for some moments contemplating Brahma's request. He could easily recover the heavens from the Asuras and return them to the gods, but he wanted to enjoy another pastime. He said, "My dear gods, please listen with great attention, for what I am about to say will bring you great fortune. Since the Asuras are presently stronger than you, you should form a truce with them."

Indra gasped. "A truce! My Lord, they are our mortal enemies."

(6.20) Vishnu replied, "Sometimes you have to make peace with your enemies to fulfil your interests."

Indra bowed his head in acquiescence, and Surya said, "How will an alliance with the Asuras help us?"

(6.21) Vishnu smiled. "Together, you will be able to produce a life-giving nectar which will make anyone who drinks it immortal."

The gods looked quizzically at each other. Brahma asked, "How are they to do that, my Lord?"

(6.22-23) Vishnu turned to Indra. "You and your companions should collect all kinds of vegetables, grass, creepers and medicinal herbs. Throw them into the Milk Ocean. Then you gods should cooperate with the Asuras to churn the ocean. You can use Mandara Mountain as your churning rod. I will also help."

"If the Asuras become immortal, they will give everyone endless grief," said Indra, frowning.

Vishnu smiled. "Have no fear. They will help with the labour, but you gods will reap the benefit."

Indra said, "They will never allow that. They are more powerful than us now. If anything, they will take all the nectar from us."

(6.24) Vishnu spoke reassuringly. "Whatever they do, do not argue with them. Be agreeable and acquiesce to all their terms."

"Is there anything else we should know?" asked Chandra.

(6.25-27) Vishnu said, "The first thing that will be generated is a poison known as Kalakuta. Do not be alarmed by that. After that, other products will manifest from the churning. Don't be greedy to get any of these, nor angry when the Asuras snatch them."

Indra said, "We should stay focused on getting the nectar."[45]

"Exactly!" said Vishnu and then disappeared from their presence.

Brahma and Shiva called out, "All glories to Lord Vishnu", and prostrated themselves in obeisance. Then they left for their abodes.

Indra and his party returned to Amaravati, which Bali now ruled. They walked in on foot, carrying baskets of fruits and flowers as offerings for the Asura king. His guards at the gates of Amaravati arrested them and took them before their leader.

(6.28-29) Bali sat surrounded by his chief commanders, shining with splendour, having conquered the universe. Seeing the gods kneeling before him, holding up their offerings, he laughed. "So Indra! You have come to accept me as your lord!"

One of the Asura generals unsheathed his sword and jumped to his feet. "My lord! It is not wise to trust these gods. Better to kill them immediately."

Other commanders snarled, "Kill the gods!" and pulled out their weapons. Bali smiled and motioned with his hand for them to sit down.

"My dear friends," he laughed, "we are great heroes, cultured rulers of the universe. Those who know religion always treat a guest with courtesy. The Devas have come without weapons and in peace."

Turning to Indra, Bali said, "Present your tribute."

Each god stepped forward in turn, placed his offering on the crystal steps below the throne and knelt before Bali, who commanded his servants to bring low seats for them.

(6.30) When they were all seated, Indra addressed Bali respectfully. "O great King Bali, you are indeed a great hero. As the son of the great Asura lord, Virochana, and the grandson of the exalted devotee Prahlada, it is not surprising that you act perfectly in accord with religious principles. Please accept these gifts from us, who are your sincere admirers."

Bali laughed and turned to his generals. "Did you hear that? My sincere admirers!"

All the Asura chiefs and soldiers laughed mockingly, but remembering Vishnu's words, the gods did not react.

"So what caused this change of heart?" asked Bali.

Indra said, "The Supersoul in the hearts of all beings, Lord Vishnu, being equal to all, desires your good. He has asked us to give up all enmity and quarrel with you and instead cooperate to produce an elixir of immortality."

(6.31) Bali summoned his chief ministers, Shambara and Arishtanemi, to come closer.

"What do you both think?" he whispered.

"Look at them!" said Shambara. "They are weak and are no match for us."

"We can use them to get the nectar and then take it all ourselves," added Arishtanemi.

"I think so too," said Bali.

(6. 32) He turned to Indra. "Very well, I agree. Now go take some rest and refreshments along with your associates. We shall set off tomorrow."

Early the next morning, Bali deployed a couple of his trusted aides to collect the various ingredients Vishnu had specified. "Meet us on the shore of the Milk Ocean," he told them.

(6.33-35) Then he, his generals and the gods rode on swift mounts to the golden base of Mandara Mountain. There, with all their strength, they worked together to uproot the vast mountain. With loud heroic cries, they laboured valorously to carry it to the milk ocean. After transporting the hill a long distance, they became exhausted. Unable to take it any further, they tried to place it down. The mountain, however, toppled over on its side, crushing many gods and Asuras to death.

(6.36) Bloodied and bruised, Bali stormed up to Indra, sitting dazed on the ground. "I should never have trusted you! You have lured us to our destruction!"

Indra stood up and, with gentle words, tried to calm Bali. "If I tricked you to your destruction, then I have done the same to myself. "Look, how many hundreds of gods lie dead."

Tears welled in his eyes. "Some of my closest companions have been crushed to death."

(6.37) Just then, the whole sky became illuminated with a brilliant light. Gods and Asuras alike shielded their eyes from the blinding effulgence. As Indra squinted up, he saw Vishnu seated on Garuda's back, surveying the damage. As his glance swept over the dead and wounded gods and Asuras, their injuries healed, and they were all revived. They rose, as if from sleep, feeling refreshed.

(6.38-39) Descending from Garuda, Vishnu quickly lifted the mountain with one hand and placed it on Garuda's back. Then accompanied by the cheering gods and Asuras, he went to the Milk Ocean. When they arrived, Vishnu commanded Garuda to place Mount Mandara by the water and then depart.

Garuda knelt before Vishnu. "Allow me to help more, my Lord."

Vishnu smiled affectionately at Garuda. "O mighty eagle, you have already accomplished what is only possible for you. Please return now to your abode. I wish the serpent king, Vasuki, to become the churning rope. If you are here, he will be reluctant to show himself."

Bowing to his Lord, Garuda spread his mighty wings and ascended to the spiritual world.

Shiva Drinks Poison

(7.1) The gods and Asuras sat on the shore of the milk ocean, intoning mantras to summon Vasuki. Impelled by the chanting, the Naga king appeared before them, and after bowing low to Vishnu, he asked the others why they had summoned him.

Indra opened his mouth to reply, but Bali interrupted. Stepping forward, he declared, "O Naga leader, know me to be King Bali, lord of the universe. On my order, coil yourself around this Mandara Mountain. I wish to use your body as a churning rope."

Vasuki hissed and recoiled from Bali. "I will not! What you ask will be arduous and may even cost me my life. I shall certainly not obey you."

Bali unsheathed his sword and raised it as if to strike Vasuki. "How dare you disobey me? You will do as I say or die at my hands this moment!"

Indra quickly edged close to Bali and quietly whispered in his ear, "My lord, we will gain nothing if you kill him. I have another idea. Please give your permission for me to address him."

Still scowling, Bali sheathed his sword and grunted his assent. Indra smiled at Vasuki and spoke gently. "Dear Vasuki, on the order of Lord Ajita,

Vishnu himself, who stands here among us, we have called you to do his will."

Vasuki glanced at Ajita and respectfully replied, "What is the Lord's will?"

"He desires the good of both gods and Asuras and has asked that we cooperate with you to churn this great ocean of milk. By so doing, we will create an elixir of immortality which we are to share."

Vasuki's eyes widened, "An elixir of immortality! Will I also get a share?"

He turned to Ajita for confirmation; the Lord smiled and nodded. Vasuki immediately coiled his gigantic body around the mountain.

(7.2) Followed by the gods, Ajita strode to Vasuki's head and grasped his front portion. Bali, piqued at being upstaged by Indra, stood with legs apart and arms folded, glowering at the gods. All the Asuras stood behind him. In friendly tones, Indra invited Bali, "My dear brother, let us take up this great task together. Please order the Asuras to seize Vasuki's tail."

(7.3) Bali's face flushed with indignation. "Most lowly Indra, how dare you order your superior? We Asuras are the rulers of the universe, accomplished scholars of the Vedas, and famous for our birth and activities. We shall not take the serpent's tail since it is inferior to his head."

(7.4) Indra's face reddened, as did the other gods'. Bali was too insolent. How could they continue to brook his insults? Vishnu, however, smiled. Releasing Vasuki's head, he walked over to his tail and picked it up. Seeing this, Indra and the other gods controlled their anger and, without another word, followed him.

(7.5-7) Smiling smugly at each other, the Asuras strode proudly to Vasuki's head. Then together with the gods, they pulled Mount Mandara into the ocean with the intent of churning it. To their dismay, the mountain sank, despite their best efforts to keep it afloat. They looked at each other with furrowed brows and shook their heads, unsure how to solve this problem.

(7.8-10) Ajita spoke reassuringly. "Do not worry. My will is always supreme." He then assumed the form of a gigantic tortoise and, entering the water, lifted the mountain on his back, which was 800,000 miles in diameter. The mountain's peak slowly emerged, with Vasuki still coiled tightly around it. The gods and Asuras, feeling encouraged, picked up his tail and head and began churning.

"Surely, this is the Lord's form as Kurma, the divine turtle," said Indra. The god became anxious that they may be causing Kurma discomfort as the mountain twisted and turned on his back, but Kurma reassured him that he was enjoying the rolling action of the mountain as a pleasant back scratch.

After labouring for many hours, the gods, Asuras and Vasuki again began to feel exhausted. Vasuki cried out, "I am dying! Please stop! I cannot take any more."[46]

(7.11) Seeing their predicament, Ajita intervened. He entered the Asuras as the energy of passion to enliven them, the gods as the energy of goodness, and Vasuki as ignorance to make him unconscious of his pain.[47]

(7.12) As they vigorously churned, the mountain wobbled from side to side. To keep it firmly in place, Ajita assumed another thousand-handed form as large as the mountain. Rising above the mountain's summit, he held it in place with one hand. On seeing this, all the gods expanded into second forms and showered him with flowers from the sky.

(7.13) Encouraged by Vishnu's help from above, below, and within themselves, the gods and Asuras strenuously re-applied themselves to churning for the nectar. Through their vigorous efforts, the Milk Ocean became agitated, and fierce sea monsters appeared on its surface, thrashing about in fear.

(7.14-15) From his thousands of mouths, Vasuki breathed smoke and blazing fire, greatly afflicting the nearby Asuras headed by Bali and his ministers, Pauloma, Kaleya, and Ilvala, who bore the brunt of the flames. Although the gods were further away from Vasuki's mouths, they were also affected by his burning breath. The strength of both gods and Asuras diminished, and their bodies became blackened. Ajita took pity on the gods, and by his grace, clouds appeared in the sky, pouring torrents of rain, and breezes carrying particles of water from the sea waves sprang up to give them relief.

(7.16-17) Still, despite Vishnu's help and their best effort, the gods and Asuras could not extract any nectar. Therefore, Ajita took hold of Vasuki's head and tail with his powerful arms, which bestow fearlessness on all beings throughout the universe. He began to churn the ocean single-handedly. As he laboured, he looked like a magnificent sapphire mountain.[48] His yellow garments flew about him, his earrings shone like lightning, his hair spread over his shoulders, and his garland swung side to side.

(7.18-20) The entire ocean became so turbulent that all the fish, sharks, tortoises and snakes became terrified, and even the large aquatics like whales, water elephants and *timingilas* were thrown to the surface. While the ocean was being churned, it produced a fiercely dangerous poison called *halahala*. The virulent black liquid began to ooze rapidly in all directions. All the Asuras took to their heels, screaming in fear. The equally panic-stricken gods, however, followed Ajita to the summit of Kailasha Hill, where Shiva sat with his wife, Bhavani. He was worshipped by great saintly persons desiring freedom from birth and death. Ajita instructed the gods to entreat the merciful Shiva to protect them. Indra and the host of gods hurriedly went forward and knelt before Shiva.

Shiva looked at them in surprise. "My dear gods, what can I do for you?"

(7.21) They said in unison, "O greatest of the gods, Mahadeva, please save us from a fiery poison which is spreading all over the three worlds."

Shiva said, "I am the destroyer. If you want protection, you should go to Lord Vishnu."[49]

(7.22) Indra replied, "O great one, since Lord Vishnu acts through you to bind or liberate conditioned souls, we accept you as the ruler of the material universe. The wise take shelter of you, knowing you can mitigate our material suffering and even give us liberation."

(7.23-24) Then all the gods together recited a prayer to Vishnu.[50] "We offer obeisance to the supreme, self-manifesting Lord who creates the material universe through his energy. He expands himself as Brahma, Vishnu, and Shiva to create, maintain and destroy it. Your effulgence is the inconceivable, impersonal Brahman, the source of both matter and the living beings.

(7.25-31) "Both the energies which bind and liberate us come from you. The planets, elements, time, etc., all constitute your universal form. You are the Supersoul, the ultimate truth, and you are celebrated as Shiva, which means most auspicious. Irreligion is your shadow, the three modes of nature are your three eyes, and the Vedic literature is your glance.[51] Your Brahman effulgence lies beyond the modes of nature and is not understood even by the three highest universal directors."

Shiva's eyes widened in indignation. "Are you suggesting that not even the omniscient Lord Vishnu understands the Brahman?"

"He is supreme, of course," said Indra! "Still, he does not need to understand what is going on in his all-pervading expansion."[52]

"What do you mean?" exclaimed Shiva.

"Not understanding the impersonal Brahman does not detract from Lord Vishnu's omniscience since it is like knowledge of a flower in the sky."[53]

Shiva still glared at the gods. How could he brook any insult to Lord Vishnu?

(7.32) Anxious to placate him, Surya said, "My lord, when flames emanate from your angry eyes to destroy the universe do you understand how that happens? Could you explain to us the process by which this occurs?"

"This is a trivial, petty task I perform routinely. I would not waste my time to understand its mechanics."

"That's what we meant by saying not even Vishnu understands the impersonal Brahman. He could if he wanted to, but it is too insignificant for him to think about."

Shiva calmed down. "Oh well, if that's what you meant, that's fine. Pray continue with your petition."

Letting out a sigh of relief, Indra continued. "My dear lord, destruction is not a problem for you. We all remember how easily you destroyed Daksha's sacrifice and many Asuras like Tripurasura, Kala and Gara.[54]

"What do you want me to destroy this time?"

"The *halahala* poison," said Indra.

"*Halahala*? What do you mean?"

"It is also called *kalakuta*," said Surya. "A very virulent poison."

"So the purpose of all this glorification is to ask me to obliterate a little poison?"

The gods looked at one another nervously. They could not tell from his tone if Shiva was annoyed with them or merely confirming he correctly understood their desire.

(7.33-35) Indra decided it would be prudent to mollify the mighty deity. He said, "Shameless people criticise you by suggesting you are ferocious, envious, or lusty. Liberated souls, however, always meditate on your sacred feet, for they know you are always engaged in severe austerity. What to speak of low-class materialists? Not even Lord Brahma and we gods can fully appreciate your greatness, for you are greater than all moving and non-moving beings. How can any of us properly glorify you? Yet, we have tried to express our appreciation according to our ability. Although we cannot fully understand your greatness, your presence enables others to flourish and be happy."

(7.36) On hearing Indra's humble petition, Shiva remembered his determination always to do others good. His demeanour softened. The gods were suffering, and his duty was to show them compassion.

(7.37-38) Turning to his wife, Shiva said, "My dear Bhavani, see how these poor souls are in great danger because of the *halahala* poison. It is my duty to protect all living entities struggling for existence. Indeed, the master must look after his suffering dependants."

Bhavani frowned. "The conditioned souls are always envious of each other. These gods are no better. They hate the Asura races. You are not like them. You are self-satisfied. You should have nothing to do with them.[55]

(7.39-40) Shiva smiled at his wife. "Conditioned souls fight each other because they are bewildered by the Lord's illusory energy. Krishna's devotees, however, are different. We try to save others, even at the risk of our own lives. In this way, my dear gentle wife, we devotees please Krishna. When Krishna is pleased, everyone becomes happy, including me. Therefore, please let me drink the poison. By my doing this, everyone will become happy."

(7.41) Bhavani smiled. "I know of your greatness and that this poison poses no personal danger to you. Therefore, I have no objection."

(7.42) Shiva then accompanied the gods to the milk ocean. They saw that the quantity of poison was so great that it spread all over the universe. Indra and the other gods became dispirited. The problem had grown to such enormous dimensions that they were wondering if even Shiva could solve it. Shiva, however, was unperturbed. Mystically he drew the entire quantity of poison into the palm of his hand and drank it. The gods gasped in wonderment. Surya said, "Lord Shiva is truly great. He can perform tasks which would destroy anyone else. I now understand why no one should try to imitate him."

(7.43-45) As they watched Shiva drink, a blue line appeared around his neck. "What's that line?" asked Indra.

The Ashvini Kumara brothers replied, "The poison must have caused it."

Ajita said, "This line will become famous as Shiva's ornament."

Then he turned to address all the gods who stood in wide-eyed admiration of Shiva. "Great personalities almost always accept voluntary suffering to relieve the miseries of others. This is considered the highest method of worshipping Lord Vishnu, who is in everyone's heart."

The gods cheered loudly, "All praise to the compassionate Lord Shiva. All praise to the Supreme Lord, Ajita!"

(7.46) Shiva wiped his hands together. A few drops of the poison fell to the ground. Some snakes and other living entities, like scorpions who accompanied him immediately took the opportunity to drink those remnants.

One of the Ashvini Kumara brothers cautioned the other gods. "Dear brothers, henceforward be wary of these species. Their bites will be most venomous."

8
Churning the Milk Ocean

(8.1) When the danger had passed, the Asuras headed by Bali said, "Let us continue with our task. The hard part is done, and soon we will enjoy the fruits of our work."

The gods picked up Vasuki's tail, and the two parties began churning with renewed vigour. Soon a celestial *surabhi* cow emerged from the foaming milk ocean.

(8.2) The great sages watching from the skies saw the cow. One said, "This cow can produce unlimited quantities of milk, yoghurt, and ghee, all of which are required for our Vedic ceremonies."

"Yes," said another. "With her ghee alone, we can perform all the sacrifices necessary for attaining Brahma's planet in our next lives."

Seeing that both the gods and Asuras were neglecting the cow, they hurried to the place and took her away.

(8.3) The gods and Asuras continued their energetic churning. Next there emerged from the frothing ocean a magnificent white war stallion.

A voice from the sky declared, "This horse is Ucchaihshrava!"

As soon as he saw it, Bali wanted it. "Only I, the undisputed ruler of the universe, deserve this fine steed!" he declared.

Remembering Ajita's advice to them, the gods did not object.

(8.4) Once he had securely tethered Ucchaihshrava, Bali gripped Vasuki's head and resumed the churning. Shortly after that, a great white elephant appeared.

The same celestial voice declared, "This is Airavata"

Everyone gasped in wonderment.

"I have never seen an elephant with four tusks!" said Chandra.

"Each tusk rivals the glories of Lord Shiva's abode, Mount Kailasha," observed Surya.

(8.5) In quick succession after Airavata emerged another eight bull and eight cow elephants. The celestial voice announced the names of the prime bull and cow of the herd as Airavana and Abhramu.

(8.6-7) The churning then produced the two divine gems, Kaustubha and Padmaraga. Ajita desired them, and they mystically alighted onto his chest. Next emerged the heavenly *parijata* flower, followed by beautiful Apsaras. However, the gods and Asuras resisted their allure and continued churning.

(8.8-10) Then another lady appeared whose beauty far exceeded that of the Apsaras. The Asuras and gods dropped Vasuki and stood gaping at her.

"Just see!" said one. "She sparkles more attractively than lightning from a crystal mountain. Who is she?"

A celestial voice announced, "Behold the Goddess of Fortune, Ramaa. She is the source of all wealth."

She looked out among the gathered assembly and indicated she would choose a husband from among them. One thought crossed everyone's mind. If she chooses me as her husband, I will become the wealthiest person in the universe.

Desiring to impress her, Indra gallantly hurried forward to offer her a suitable seat. All the sacred rivers, including the Ganges and Yamuna, appeared in their personified forms with golden waterpots for her worship.

One by one, other celestials came forward with paraphernalia used in worship.

(8.11-16) The earth goddess arrived bearing suitable herbs. Celestial cows provided ample milk and other necessities. The deity of spring brought many fragrant flowers. When everything was assembled, the sages performed the ritual bathing ceremony for the goddess as directed by the Vedic scriptures.

Meanwhile, Gandharvas and Apsaras danced and sang in praise of her, and the personified clouds played various drums, blew conch shells and bugles, and played flutes and stringed instruments. Airavata and the other sixteen elephants used their trunks to bathe the goddess. While being bathed, she looked exquisitely beautiful, holding a lotus flower. The gods then came forward and offered her gifts.

(8.17) When her worship was complete, she rose from her seat, holding a garland of lotus flowers, and began moving among the many gods and Asuras vying for her attention. Smiling shyly, her cheeks decorated with earrings, she looked gorgeous.

(8.18) The Asuras breathed heavily. One muttered under his breath, "I have never seen such symmetrical breasts!"

Another said, "Just see how she has smeared them with sandalwood and *kunkuma* powder."

The gods also admired her openly. "Just the tinkling of her ankle bells as she walks here and there is stealing my mind," said one.

Another said, "She resembles a golden creeper."

(8.19-20) Unheedful of such comments, the goddess walked among them, scrutinising each of them in search of a suitable husband. Durvasa boasted, "O goddess, choose me. I have undergone great austerity."[56]

She shook her head. "You have not yet conquered anger."

Brihaspati called out, "Choose me; I possess great knowledge."

She shook her head. "You are still a victim of material desires."

Brahma declared, "I am a great personality; surely I am fit to be your husband."

She shook her head. "You have not defeated lust."

The Asuras crowded around her, jostling for her attention.

Turning away from them, she announced, "I cannot take shelter of one who is not free of faults. Furthermore, since all of you are controlled by something, you are not yourselves the supreme controller."

The sages and gods hoped they had more chance and began calling out to her. "I am not like the others. Choose me."

(8.21) The goddess shook her head. Pointing to Shukra, she said, "I know you possess full knowledge of religion, but I also know you are not friendly toward all living beings."[57]

Then she swept her arm to encompass them all. "I realise many of you gods are somewhat renounced, but not enough to be saved from repeated birth and death. Many of you are very powerful, yet none can check the all-powerful influence of time."

One suitor protested, "I have fully renounced attachment to the material world."

The goddess again shook her head. "You cannot compare to the Supreme Person. None of you is completely free from the influence of the three modes of nature."

Bali tried to woo her, promising to protect her throughout his long life.

(8.22-23) She turned away from him. "I know you are extremely long-lived Bali, but what is the use of that? You are bereft of good conduct due to your Asuric nature."

Manu's sons called out, "Choose one of us. Our conduct is impeccable."

"Maybe," she replied. "But as humans, your life span is short."

Some of Shiva's ghostly followers called out, "Choose our lord. He is both long-lived and pious."

"That is true," agreed the goddess. "But his behaviour is inauspicious."

"How can you say that?" they challenged.

"Does he not like spending time in crematoriums? This is not very appealing behaviour."

Then she turned her eyes on Ajita, who alone was not seeking her attention, and said, "One who is actually auspicious is not eager to possess me.[58] I have therefore decided to accept Lord Ajita, the bestower of liberation, as my husband."

The Asuras protested, "Why are you interested in him? He is indifferent to you."

"I choose him because he alone is happy with or without me. Furthermore, he possesses all transcendental qualities and mystic powers. Therefore, I desire him alone as my husband."

(8.24) With these words, she walked toward Ajita and placed her garland of newly grown lotus flowers over his head. Then smiling shyly, she waited by his side. Knowing her mind, Ajita allowed her to take her place on his chest, unseen by others.[59]

(8.25) The gods cheerfully accepted her choice. Brahma told the others, "Ajita is the Supreme Lord, the father of the three worlds. His chest is the Goddess of Fortune's natural resting place."

The other gods cheered, "All glory to Lakshmi-Narayana!"

The goddess, pleased by the gods' worship of her husband, blessed them to regain their opulence.

(8.26-27) The Gandharvas and Charanas, along with their wives, broke out in ecstatic singing and dancing. The rhythmic sound of their musical instruments and conch shells created a festive atmosphere. Brahma, Shiva, Sage Angira and the administrative gods became enthused by the positive energy. They showered flowers on the divine couple and recited mantras glorifying them.

(8.28) Lakshmi was delighted, and she blessed the celestials with good behaviour and transcendental qualities, at which they displayed great happiness.

(8.29) The Asuras, neglected by the Goddess of Fortune, became depressed and frustrated. They shamelessly called out, "Let us abduct her! Who can stop us? We are the undisputed rulers of the universe!"

They drew their swords, but the gods intercepted them. Bali could see that to reach the Goddess Lakshmi they would have to kill the gods.

But then who would help them get the nectar of immortality? He checked his men. "Let us first get the elixir, my friends. Do not let a woman distract us from our goal."

Begrudgingly the Asuras sheathed their weapons and again took up Vasuki's head.

(8.30) As the gods and Asuras churned furiously, from the foamy ocean arose the lotus-eyed goddess of intoxication, Varuni. She glanced seductively at the Daityas.

"This one is ours!" declared Bali.

Remembering Ajita's earlier instruction to them, the gods did not protest.

(8.31-33) When she took her place at Bali's side, the two parties resumed churning. Then from the frothy milk, a superb male appeared. He seemed like a powerful young lion with long, sinewy arms adorned with bangles. His neck, marked with three lines, resembled a conch shell and his eyes were reddish. Of blackish complexion, he was dressed in yellow garments, decorated with various ornaments, and garlanded with flowers. In his hand, he held a large jug filled with nectar.

(8.34) A voice from the sky announced, "This is Dhanvantari. He is a plenary part of a plenary portion of Lord Vishnu and is fully conversant with the science of medicine. He may enjoy a share of all sacrifices along with the gods."

(8.35-36) Bali immediately realised Dhanvantari's jug contained the elixir.

"Get that vessel!" he commanded as he leapt forward to wrestle it from Dhanvantari.

The other Asuras swiftly surrounded Dhanvantari, and before the gods could do anything to stop them, they raced off with it.

The gods stood in shocked surprise. Everything had happened so fast. What should they do? The Asuras were already far away; they would never catch them. Feeling dispirited, they turned to Ajita for help.

(8.37) Ajita reassured them. "Do not be aggrieved dear gods. By my energy, I shall bewilder the Asuras and make them quarrel. Thus, I shall fulfil your desire to have the nectar."

(8.38) Meanwhile, the Asuras, having put a great distance between themselves and the gods, had stopped in a quiet and secluded place.

Bali instructed his generals to keep watch in case the gods tried to ambush them before they could all drink the elixir.

They replied, "Well, let us have a drink first, then we'll keep watch while the rest of you drink."

"What?" said Bali. "I am the king here; I drink first. Now do as you are told and go stand watch."

"What's the objection? Why can't we first take a quick swig?"

"Because I am the king."

"Well, I am your chief general, so I should be the second to drink. Send someone else to stand watch."

Bali reluctantly agreed, but the other generals also demanded that they should be among the first to drink. "Send the foot soldiers to stand guard."

The Asura soldiers protested, fearing the generals would finish all the elixir and not leave any for them.

(8.39-40) "Why should any of us go and stand guard? The gods helped churn the Milk Ocean; they are also entitled to some. Let's wait for them to come, and Ajita can fairly share the elixir."

"How dare you tell me what to do?" shouted Bali.

"We are merely reminding you of the agreement you made."

They argued back and forth among themselves. In the meantime, the gods and Ajita caught up with them.

Spotting the bickering Asuras, Indra turned to Ajita. "What should we do?"

"Just wait here and leave everything to me."

(8.41-46) Before the astonished eyes of the gods, he assumed the form of a voluptuous woman. Her complexion resembled a fresh blackish lotus. Each of her limbs was beautifully formed. Her ears were decorated with earrings, her cheeks radiant, her nose gently raised, her breasts were large, and her waist thin. Her demeanour was youthful and very pleasing to the minds of all who beheld her. Her attractive bodily fragrance, made even more alluring by the scent of her *mallika* flower garland, attracted bumble bees. Her legs were decorated with ankle bells, her sari was clean, and she was tastefully decorated with celestial jewels.

The gods stared at her in wide-eyed wonder. "Who are you?"

"This feminine incarnation of mine will be renowned as Mohini-murti, the Enchantress."

Mohini turned and walked to where the Asuras were still squabbling among themselves. Hearing her ankle bells, they turned to see who was coming. Their mouths fell open, and they stood motionless as she approached. When she moved her eyebrows and smiled shyly, their hearts filled with a burning desire to possess her.

9
Vishnu Becomes a Woman

(9.1-2) The Asuras' attention became transfixed on the beautiful girl approaching them. They stopped brawling over the pot of nectar and gaped at her.

"I have never seen anyone so beautiful!" sighed one.

"Me neither!" chorused the others.

(9.3) Straightening out their clothes and tousled hair, they tried to cut a suave and dashing pose.

"O most beautiful girl," called out one, "your eyes resemble lotus petals."

Another crooned, "Who are you, dear one? Where do you come from?"

"My name is Mohini," said the girl shyly.

Another Asura forcefully pushed in front of the others and, smoothing down his hair, silkily said, "If you desire a husband, Mohini, look no further. Here I am."

Still another elbowed him aside. "Just see those perfect thighs!"

Pushing him away, another Asura thrust out his chest and said, "Ignore him; he's crude and uncultured. Who's your father, sweetheart? Since you have stolen my mind, I will ask him for your hand in marriage."

Mohini giggled. "How do you know I am not already married?"

(9.4) "I am a highly cultured man. If you were married, my mind could not have entertained the idea of approaching you."

"Anyway," said another, "It's obvious from your demeanour that you are not yet wed."

"How can you be certain?" asked the girl in honeyed tones.

"Ooh! We can tell, all right," said another. "Why! I bet neither human, Asura, nor celestial has ever touched you. I can tell these things, you know."

(9.5) Another Asura jostled his way forward. "You are a real beauty, Mohini! Your eyebrows bewitch me. Without a doubt, Providence has sent you to captivate our minds and senses."

Mohini smiled coyly. "I came because I wanted to watch your game. What are you playing?"

The Asuras glared at one another. "We are not exactly playing."

"We were having a slight disagreement," said another Asura.

"Yes," snarled a third. "Over which of us should live or die."

Mohini covered her mouth and said in shock, "This is no place for a woman. I shall leave immediately."

Mohini glanced at the gods, who stood some distance away, smiling broadly to see her antics. "Perhaps I should go over to them. They seem a friendly bunch."

(9.6) Mohini made as if to move away, and the Asuras punched the one who had frightened her. "Beautiful Mohini," said Bali, "there is no reason to be afraid. This is nothing serious. We are all family. We were just squabbling over this pot of nectar."

He held up the pot for her to see. "We all respect you. Why don't you settle our dispute?"

Mohini looked uncertainly from the Asuras to the gods. "I think I would feel safer with them."

(9.7) "Oh, they are our brothers," said Bali.

"Really?" asked Mohini incredulously.

"Yes, Sage Kashyapa is the father of us all."

"We weren't going to kill each other. We were showing off our strength. It's what men do."

"You said you were quarrelling."

"Just a minor dispute. Nothing that cannot be easily resolved. You can settle the matter by dividing the nectar equally among us."

(9.8-9) Mohini looked thoughtful as if she was considering the Asuras' suggestion. Twirling her long braids with her delicate hands, she smiled seductively at them. "You won't have such faith in me when you find out I am a prostitute."

They all gulped. What a fine turn of events! They could enjoy her to their hearts' content if they could persuade her to stay with them.

Bali said, "We are men of our word. As we have said, we will accept your judgement; we will do so regardless of who or what you are."

Mohini arched her eyebrows. "Really? You are the learned Kashyapa's sons, so how can you trust a loose woman?"

"Ah!" said one of the Asuras, "we are a good judge of character. We can tell that at heart you are pure."[60]

"Yes," said another. "You are just testing our love for you."

Eager to impress her, many of them spoke at once.

"A real prostitute would pretend to be chaste."

"We can tell that you are quite unsullied."

"Only a uniquely pure woman would be so honest as to admit past misdeeds."

"Even so," said Mohini with a giggle, "a truly learned person would never put his faith in a woman."

"Why not?" asked Bali.

(9.10) She laughed. "My dear Asuras, I am here without a chaperone.[61] Do the learned not say that friendship with women like me is never permanent? They compare us to monkeys and jackals who continually seek new sexual partners. Isn't that so?"

(9.11) Thinking she was joking, the Asuras laughed and slapped each other's backs. "You are hilarious," said Bali. "We are not so foolishly chauvinistic." They all laughed and nodded their assent.

Another said, "We judge people by their character, not by their sex."

"We are confident of your integrity," said Bali. He placed the pot of nectar in her hands. "Here, take this and do as you deem fit. You may drink it, divide it among us, or throw it away. We will accept whatever choice you make."[62]

(9.12) Mohini smiled and looked up innocently at the eager Asuras surrounding her. "You say that now, but what if I make a mistake? Then you will become angry with me and accuse me of cheating."

The Asuras looked at her in mock shock. "Become angry with you? Never! Not only are we good judges of character, but we are also men of our word."

"Well," said Mohini, feigning hesitancy. "If you promise you won't become angry and later accuse me of dishonesty, then maybe I could consider accepting this heavy responsibility."

(9.13) Bali said, "We understand your concern, and we promise we will accept your decision without argument." His followers shouted their approval.

Hearing them from a distance, the gods chuckled and said to one another, "What fools!"

(9.14-15) To show Mohini his righteousness, Bali called all the gods and Asuras to gather around. "My dear brothers," he said. "Partaking of this nectar is a most auspicious event. As with all such occasions, we shall observe a fast until the appropriate time set by the brahmins. According to custom, we may then take our baths and don new garments, after which we shall take our place on mats of *kusha* grass near the sacrificial fire as the brahmins offer oblations of ghee into the flames. Before receiving our share of the nectar, we shall each give charity to the cows, brahmins and other members of society. Are we in agreement?"

Both gods and Asuras shouted out their approval.

(9.16-17) The next day, after the rituals were completed, the gods and Asuras awaited Mohini's arrival. They sat facing east in the sacrificial arena, which was decorated with flower garlands and lamps and made fragrant by burning sticks of incense. They could hear her tinkling ankle bells behind them as she slowly approached the arena. Turning around to see her, their mouths fell open in awe of her beauty. She had dressed in a most attractive sari, which hugged her big low hips, large breasts and beautiful thighs. Her eyes darted in youthful playfulness from one to the other as she slowly approached, holding the waterpot in her hands.

(9.18) As she drew closer, they became mesmerised by her attractive nose and cheeks, beautified by her dangling earrings. When she entered their midst, her sari's border, which had been covering her breasts, slipped off. She pulled it back with a shy glance toward the gods and Asuras, who sat with mouths agape, utterly enchanted.

(9.19-20) The Asuras sat up straight, flexing their muscles to impress her. Mohini, however, knew they were cruel by nature and to give them the nectar would be like feeding milk to a serpent. She asked them to rearrange their sitting places to ensure they did not get any.

"Let the Asuras sit here in a line, and the gods can please go over there. Please arrange yourselves according to your seniority."

She waited as they rearranged themselves.

(9.21) When they were seated, Mohini approached the Asuras. "I was observing you all and concluded that the Asuras are nobler than the gods, who are far less disciplined than you heroes. Just see how disturbed they are, seeing me with you."

The Asuras nodded vigorously. Bali said, "Yes. Discipline is what we have in abundance and what our weak brothers over there lack."

"I can see that," said Mohini. "You are all men of your word. The gods seem agitated and about to start a fight. If they do I will surely flee this place."

Adopting a conspiratorial tone, she whispered, "I will pacify them by giving them a small share, and then you may have the rest. Unlike yourselves, they don't seem to understand that good things come to those who wait patiently."[63]

The Asuras puffed out their chests, eagerly drinking in her praise, which seemed more desirable than the nectar itself.[64]

Mohini slowly walked toward the line of gods.

One of the lesser Asuras whispered to the others, "Is it wise to let the gods drink before us?"

Another said, "It doesn't seem fair to me."

Bali and his chief generals scowled disapprovingly at them.

(9.22-23) "We have given our word to accept whatever she does, fair or otherwise," said Bali.

One of his generals added, "Do you want us to lose our prestige by fighting with a woman?"

"Well, no, but maybe…."

"No buts," said Bali firmly. "She obviously likes us as much as we like her. There is no need for us to ruin this affectionate relationship. I, for one, trust her and intend to show her respect by honouring her decision."

All the chief generals grunted their agreement, and the two dissenters were silenced.

(9.24) Among the Asuras was Rahu, who causes solar and lunar eclipses. He also suspected Mohini's intentions, but when he saw how the other two dissenters were silenced, he quietly assumed the guise of a god and slipped unnoticed into their line. Mohini passed down the row of gods, pouring nectar into their goblets, including his. However, when he raised his cup to drink, the sun and moon gods, who had a long-lasting feud with Rahu, recognised him.

"Stop him!" they shouted. "He is the demon Rahu."

(9.25-26) Before the nectar could travel further than Rahu's throat, Mohini summoned the Sudarshana disc and cut off his head. Since the nectar had reached his neck, his severed head remained alive, suspended in space, but his body fell lifeless to the floor. Rahu's disembodied face distorted into an anguished howl. The gods quickly consumed their portions of nectar while the bewildered Asuras stared in their direction, trying to determine what was causing the commotion.

(9.27-28) Mohini then resumed her original form as Ajita. The gods loudly sang his praise. "All glories to the Supreme Personality of Godhead, the best friend and well-wisher of the three worlds."

The Asuras fumed. "We have been cheated!"

"This is unfair," protested Bali. "We all worked equally hard but have not all reaped the same result."

Ajita said, "You Asuras have never understood that only by taking shelter of me, the Supreme Personality of Godhead, can anyone succeed. Not knowing this, you have failed."

Bali angrily retorted, "We did not deserve this treachery. How have we differed from the gods?"

(9.29) Ajita replied, "Everyone works to protect their wealth and life, but if they do not also engage in my devotional service, they are baffled. However, the same activities are successful when done for my pleasure. Such work benefits everyone, just as water poured on the root of a tree is distributed throughout its entirety."

10
The Battle.

(10.1-2) The Asuras jumped up, shouting at Ajita. "We have been deceived. You should have given us an equal share of the nectar."

Ajita spoke calmly. "I churned the ocean and produced the nectar only to help the gods because, unlike you Asuras, they are my dear devotees."

Ajita then summoned Garuda and, mounting him, returned to his abode

(10.3) The Asuras were infuriated. "We will not tolerate this injustice!"

Raising their weapons, they advanced menacingly on the gods. "Attack them! Slay them all! Spare none!"

(10.4) The gods, rejuvenated by the nectar, drew their weapons and prepared to defend themselves. Indra reassured them, "Remember Lord Narayana. He is always our shelter."

(10.5-15) The two formidable parties clashed in a fury, giving full vent to their long-standing mutual hostility. Conch shells, bugles, drums and trumpets combined with the cries of elephants and horses to create a tumultuous uproar. The Asura warriors were mounted on diverse carriers. Some rode on the backs of camels, some on huge monkeys, some on tigers and some on lions. Others sat astride vultures, eagles, hawks and geese. Warriors charged into the fray riding buffalo, rhinos, bulls, lizards, goats, deer and boars. Some were even mounted upon reptiles like crocodiles and massive shark-faced lizards, while others rode upon the fantastic *timingila* whale.

Bellowing in anger, the combatants closed upon each other. They appeared like two oceans colliding. The infantry fought other infantry, while the cavalry confronted those fighters on the opposing side. Decorated with jewelled canopies and umbrellas, with colourful banners flying from poles of crystal and lapis lazuli, their burnished armours shining brilliantly and their silver and gold shields reflecting the sunlight, the combined armies were dazzling.

Celestial sages, watching from the sky, remarked, "We have never seen such fierce fighting. Just hearing about this battle will make people's hair stand erect."

(10.16-18) "Just see," said another sage. "The Daitya king, Bali, son of Virochana, is seated on a wonderful aeroplane. Sometimes he is visible, and then suddenly, he vanishes."

"Ah, yes," said another. "This plane is the celebrated Vaihayasa, made by the Asura Maya. It is equipped with all types of weapons. Its powers are inconceivable and indescribable."

Another sage said, "See how majestic Bali looks seated under its protective umbrella, fanned by an excellent *chamara* and surrounded by his captains and commanders!"

"Yes! He resembles the moon rising in the evening, illuminating all directions."

(10.19-24) The first sage asked, "Who are those powerful heroes seated on chariots surrounding the Vaihayasa?"

His companion replied, "They are Bali's powerful commanders and captains. See that is Namuchi; there is Shambara, Bana, Viprachitti, Ayonmukha, Dvimurdha, Kalanabha, Praheti, Heti, Ilvala, Shakuni, Bhutasatapa, Vajradamshtra, Virochana, Hayagriva, Shankushira, Kapila Meghadundubhi, Taraka, Cakradrik, Shumbha, Nishumbha, Jambha, Utkala, Arishta, Arishtanemi, Tripuradhipa, and Maya. Over there are the sons of Puloma, and there you see the Kaleyas. Over there, ride the Nivatakavacha."

Another sage said, "I have never seen them so furious!"

"It's understandable," said a third. "After all, they worked hard to attain the nectar only to be denied their share."

As the sages spoke among themselves, the Asuras blew on their conch shells, making a tumultuous sound like lions roaring. "Attack! Attack!" screamed the Asura commanders. "Spare none!"

Seeing his rivals bent on the gods' destruction, Indra became furious.

(10.25) The sages' attention went to him. "Look!" said one, pointing at Indra. "There is the king of heaven, seated on his elephant, Airavata. He looks like the sun rising above Mount Udayagiri, with its countless waterfalls."

His companion said, "His great elephant can go anywhere in the universe."

"Indeed," said another sage, "and it carries a reserve of water to shower upon Indra."

"Wine, too," said another, with a chuckle.[65]

(10.26) As the sages observed the scene, Vayu, Agni, Varuna and other rulers of various planets, along with their associates, rallied around Indra to support him.

"They look very splendid," said a sage. "See how their various vehicles are decorated with flags and armed with so many weapons."

(10.27) As they watched, Bali and his party met with Indra and his party. The Asuras harshly rebuked the gods. "You pose as virtuous men, but you are just cheats and liars! Now you shall pay for your crimes."

The gods laughed in derision. "You are the criminals! You think yourselves noble but exhibit harsh and sinful behaviour."

(10.28-34) As the two enraged parties traded insults, they closed on one another. They fought in pairs, with Indra facing Bali, Kartikeyya against Taraka, Varuna fighting Heti and Yamaraja contending with Kalanabha. The god Aparajita fought with Namuchi, and the Ashvini Kumara twins stood against Vrishaparva. The sun-god faced Bali's hundred sons whom Bana headed, and the moon-god fought with Rahu, his constant enemy. The wind god came against Puloma, and Shumbha and Nishumbha tackled the supremely powerful material energy, Bhadrakali. Shiva fought Jambha, and Vibhavasu battled Mahishasura. Ilvala, along with his brother Vatapi, fought the sons of Brahma. Durmarsha fought with Cupid, the Asura Utkala with the Matrika goddesses, Brihaspati with Shukra, and Sanaischara or Saturn with Narakasura. The Maruts fought the Nivatakavacha, the Vasus fought the Kalakeya Asuras, the Vishvadeva gods fought the Pauloma Asuras, and the Rudras fought the ever-angry Krodhavasha Asuras.

(10.35-37) From all sides resounded cries of "Victory! Victory!" "Slay them all!" Weapons collided thunderously; arrows hissed through the air, and severed heads thudded to the ground. Brandished here and everywhere were firearms, disks, clubs, spears, tridents, pikes, firebrands, barbed darts, hatchets, swords, iron clubs, hammers and javelins.[66] The ground was strewn with the mutilated bodies of elephants, horses, charioteers, infantry soldiers, and many other types of mounts and their riders. Limbless trunks, shorn of their ornaments and armour, lay interspersed among a medley of severed arms, thighs, necks, legs, flags and broken weapons.

(10.38-40) As the soldiers and chariots of both armies rushed this way and that, a great dust cloud flew violently into the air covering all of outer space and completely obscuring the sun. Mixing with the continuous gushing of blood from slain heroes, it fell again to the earth, revealing a terrible sight. Decapitated heads of heroes with staring eyes and gritted teeth were scattered in every direction, interspersed with dismembered arms still clutching various weapons, and dismembered bloodied legs and thighs resembling elephant trunks. Here and there ran decapitated bodies. Having become ghosts, they continued to attack enemy soldiers, holding their heads in one hand and weapons in another.

(10.41-48) Bali fired a steady stream of arrows at Indra, Airavata, its driver and the four horsemen guarding the elephant's legs. Indra smiled as he deftly countered those arrows with shafts of his own. Bali could not bear to witness Indra's military expertise. Unable to restrain his anger, he took up his Shakti weapon, which blazed like a great firebrand. Indra instantly cut that weapon to pieces while it was still in Bali's hand. Utterly incensed, Bali hurled many other missiles at Indra in swift succession, but the gallant god also destroyed these. Bali disappeared and resorted to demonic illusions and mystic power.

An immense mountain appeared above the gods raining down blazing trees and stone slabs with jagged edges. Falling in great showers, they smashed the gods' heads. This was followed by a rain of scorpions, serpents and other poisonous creatures, lions, tigers, bears and elephants. Thousands of naked Asuras bearing great tridents appeared, crying out, "Cut them to pieces! Pierce them!"

(10.49-51) Fierce gales drove huge black clouds across the sky. With crashes of thunder, they showered down live coals. Bali invoked a devastating fire that swept across the field, scorching the gods' soldiers. This fire, accompanied by blasting winds, seemed as terrible as the Samvartaka fire, which appears at the time of dissolution. After that, whirlpools and tidal waves sprang up on all sides, causing a fearful inundation.

(10.52-55) The gods became overpowered and dispirited as the invisible Asuras unleashed these and many other magical attacks. Not seeing any way of defending themselves against these mystical weapons, they wholeheartedly meditated on Vishnu, the all-powerful creator of the universe. The lotus-eyed Vishnu immediately appeared seated on the back of Garuda with various weapons in his eight hands and destroyed the Asuras' illusions. The gods cheered loudly. "All glory to Lord Vishnu. Simply by remembering you, one becomes free from all dangers."

(10.56) Kalanemi was the first Asura warrior to notice that Vishnu, seated on Garuda, had entered the fray. Mounted on a great lion, he whirled his trident and flung it at Garuda's head. Vishnu caught the weapon in his left hand,[67] flung it back at Kalanemi, instantly killing him and his lion carrier.

(10.57) Unable to brook this, the powerful Asura generals Mali and Sumali simultaneously attacked Vishnu. In an instant, the Sudarshana discus severed both their heads. Witnessing their death, the Asura named Malyavan, roaring like a lion, attacked Vishnu. Whirling his spiked club, he first targeted Garuda, but before he could release his weapon, Vishnu's *chakra* weapon severed his head.

11
Indra Destroys the Asuras.

(11.1) Seated on Garuda, Vishnu flew across the battlefield, surveying the gods' corpses. By his glance he brought them back to life. Enlivened by their Lord's mystic potency, the rejuvenated celestials, headed by Indra and Vayu, charged the Asura hordes and drove them back.

(11.2) Expertly guiding Airavata through the carnage, Indra searched for Bali while cutting down the remaining Asura soldiers. Bali became infuriated to see Indra devastate his forces, and he raced forward to thwart the massacre. Fearing that the enraged Indra would kill their king, the Asura soldiers cried, "Alas! Alas!"

(11.3-6) Bali, confident that he was well equipped for the battle, fearlessly confronted Indra. Clutching his thunderbolt in hand, Indra loudly rebuked Bali. "Foolish Bali, do you think you can rob us gods with your magic tricks like a magician deceives a child? Do you not know that we gods are masters of all mystic powers? You are an unqualified scoundrel trying to force your way into the upper planetary systems by dint of your mystic powers. I cast fools like you to the lowest region of the universe. Despite your magic tricks, I, powerful Indra, shall today cut off your head with my sharp-edged thunderbolt. If you can, try to fight me along with your allies."

(11.7-10) Bali censured Indra in turn. "Time alone determines victory and defeat. Thus, the wise do not lament in loss or rejoice in victory. Your pride exposes you as a fool, Indra. Saintly persons pity you gods because you ignorantly take credit for your victories. Thus, although you wish to hurt me, I do not take your harsh words to heart."

Bali then fired a volley of arrows at Indra.

(11.11-12) Indra smiled tightly. Bali had a point, but that would not save him. The god hurled his infallible thunderbolt, striking Bali in the chest. The Asura king fell lifeless, and his aircraft hurtled to the ground like a mountain with its wings torn off.

(11. 13-15) Jambhasura roared in grief and fury. Desiring to avenge his friend, he urged his lion carrier to rush Indra. Jambhasura forcefully struck Indra and Airavata with his powerful club in the fierce attack. Reeling from the blow, Airavata collapsed to his knees and then toppled unconscious.

(11.16) Matali was nearby on Indra's chariot. He dexterously urged its thousand steeds forward, and Indra leapt aboard.

(11.17-18) Jambhasura shouted, "Bravo! Bravo Matali! Although I admire your bravery, I cannot spare your life."

With all his might, he threw a blazing trident at Matali, striking him on his shoulder. Matali reeled, his face contorted in pain, but kept hold of the reins and expertly guided the chariot. Indra angrily hurled his thunderbolt at Jambhasura and severed his head.

(11.19-20) Narada had been watching the battle from the skies. He knew that Jambhasura's closest friends and relatives were not involved in the fight.

They needed to be told of his death. Then they could no doubt follow him to the next world. Best get rid of all the troublesome Asuras as soon as possible. The sage hurried to their abode, where he saw Namuchi, Bala and Paka leisurely passing their time, unaware of the battle. When the three Asuras heard the news of Jambhasura's death, they quickly donned their armour and hurried to the battlefield. Ignoring the other gods, they scoured the field, looking for Indra. As soon as they spotted him, they showered him with torrents of arrows, rebuking him with harsh and cruel words.

(11.21-24) While Bala simultaneously pierced Indra's one thousand horses with an equal number of arrows, Paka released two hundred shafts smashing the chariot and severely wounding Matali. The Asura soldiers cheered as Namuchi bore down on Indra, injuring him with fifteen golden-feathered arrows that boomed like thunderclaps. Enlivened by this turn of events, many other Asura generals collectively bore down on Indra, covering him as clouds cover the sun in the rainy season.

(11.25) When the other gods, whom the Asura soldiers were relentlessly oppressing, could no longer see Indra, they became most anxious. "Alas!" they lamented. "Without a leader, we are surely doomed!"

(11.26) Indra, however, valiantly released himself from the network of arrows engulfing him. His flag fluttered triumphantly, and his thousand horses pulled with renewed vigour as Matali expertly steered his chariot. The gods sighed with relief to see their leader emerging, radiant like the rising sun.

(11.27-28) Indra surveyed the battlefield, and seeing his army sorely beleaguered by the enemy, he became furious. Determined to kill his foes, he raised his thunderbolt and hurled it at Bala and Paka, severing their heads. Their followers trembled in fear and wailed, "Alas! Who can stop Indra?"

(11.29-30) Namuchi saw his relatives fall and, howling with grief and anger, rushed at Indra, determined to kill him. Roaring like a lion, Namuchi released an ornamented steel spear. "Die, Indra! Die!"

(11.31) Indra turned just in time to see the deadly spear streaking toward him like a blazing meteor. He at once fired several arrows and cut the weapon to pieces. Taking up his thunderbolt, he hurled it at Namuchi's neck.

(11.32) To Indra's shock and dismay, the thunderbolt did not even scratch Namuchi's skin.

"How is this possible," he exclaimed. "Previously, my thunderbolt slew the stupendous Vritrasura.[68] Yet despite hurling it with all my force, it has not even slightly harmed Namuchi."

(11.33) A shiver of fear ran down Indra's spine. How had the Asura resisted his most potent weapon? Might he possess some miraculous superpower?

Indra turned pale. Surya, who was nearby, called out, "What's wrong, Indra?"

(11.34) Indra said, "Do you remember the flying mountains of long ago? How they would fall to the ground killing many people, so I used my thunderbolt to cut off their wings?"

"Yes, of course," replied Surya. "Why?"

(11.35) "I even killed Vritrasura, who was empowered with Tvasta's austerity. Indeed, I have killed many stalwart, unstoppable heroes with my thunderbolt."

"This is hardly the time for reminiscing, Indra," replied Surya. "What's your point?"

(11.36) Indra looked at him in bafflement. "Namuchi is an insignificant general among the

Asuras. Why is it my thunderbolt has been ineffectual against him?"

"Don't give up so quickly!" urged Surya. "Try again!"

Indra shook his head. "I used to think of my thunderbolt as equal to Lord Brahma's weapon, but I now see it as useless as an ordinary stick. I shall not hurl it again."

Surya persisted. "You can't just give up. Our forces will lose all heart."

(11.37-38) Indra sank to the chariot's floor, holding his head in his hand. Suddenly a voice boomed out from above. "Protected by my boon, Namuchi cannot be killed by anything dry or moist."

Indra and the gods looked around but could not see the source of the voice, which continued, "Indra, you must find another way to kill him."

(11.39-40) Indra became hopeful. The Asura was not indestructible. He just had to find a weapon which was neither dry nor moist. He thought at once of foam. That was neither dry nor moist. Chanting the appropriate mantras, he summoned a mystical foam weapon and hurled it at Namuchi, severing his head.

Surya applauded him. "Bravo, Indra!"

Greatly relieved, the sages observing the battle from above showered Indra with flowers, and some even descended to garland him.

(11.41) Vishvavasu and Paravasu, two chief Gandharvas, could be heard singing in great joy while other celestials beat drums. Many beautiful Apsaras appeared in the skies, dancing jubilantly.

(11.42) Vayu, Agni, Varuna and the other gods fought with renewed vigour, cutting down their opponents like lions killing deer.

(11.43) Watching from the skies, Brahma became concerned that the gods would annihilate the Asuras to a man. He called Narada. "Go there immediately and tell Indra to stop the fight."

(11.44) Descending swiftly, Narada hovered just above the combatants. "Stop fighting! Cease!"

Indra and the other gods looked up in surprise, their weapons raised, while the remaining Asuras quickly fled.

"Why?" asked Indra. "We are winning!"

Narada called back, "All of you gods are protected by Narayana. By his grace, you have already drunk the nectar of immortality. The goddess of fortune has also blessed you to enjoy prosperity. You do not need to kill all the Asuras. They pose no further threat to you."

(11.45) Indra conferred with Surya and the other chief gods. They decided that since Narada was Krishna's pure devotee, it was best to obey him. Sheathing their weapons, they returned to Amaravati, followed by a host of Gandharvas and Apsaras celebrating their victory.

(11.46-47) Spotting Bali lying mortally wounded on the battlefield, Narada hurried after his few surviving soldiers. "Stop fleeing! There is no more danger!"

When they finally stopped, Narada ordered them to return to the battlefield.

"Your king, Bali, is in a precarious condition. Carry him immediately to Astagiri Hill. You will find Shukra there. He will restore him to health. Indeed, take all the slain warriors who have not lost their heads and limbs, and he will revive them with the Sanjivani, a mantra known only to him."

(11.48) A few days later, by Shukra's grace, Bali was fully recovered, and he remembered all that had occurred. He visited the bedsides of some of his recuperating generals, only to find them depressed about their defeat at the gods' hands. Bali shook his head disapprovingly. "My dear Asuras, why are you lamenting so? Have you understood anything about universal affairs? Don't you know that nothing happens without the Supreme Lord's sanction?"

***

Parikit sat in enthralled silence. Truly, Krishna's activities were astonishing. Although he can do everything without effort, to enjoy pastimes with his devotees and to teach us valuable lessons, he arranges such grand dramas.

Parikit asked Shukadeva, "My lord, pray tell me what happened to Rahu's disembodied head after he sipped a drop of the celestial elixir?"

"Ah yes, Rahu's head!" said the sage with a smile. "Touched by the nectar, it became immortal. Lord Brahma, therefore, accepted it as a planet. Since Rahu is an eternal enemy of the sun and moon, he always tries to attack them on the nights of the full and dark moons."

12
Lord Shiva Bewildered

(12.1-2) After drinking the poison from the milk ocean, Shiva had retired to his abode and had not witnessed Mohini's appearance. Later, Narada laughingly told him how she had tricked the Asuras, and he became curious.

"Lord Vishnu as a woman! Is this true? I have never heard of such a thing."

"It is true," said Narada. "Vishnu's form as Mohini is even more beautiful than the Goddess of Fortune. He completely bewildered the Asuras into letting the gods drink the nectar first. It was such an enchanting pastime."

Shiva stood up. "I must see this form for myself!"

Turning to his wife, he said, "My dear Devi, if you wish, you may come with me."

Uma rose gracefully from her seat, "I, too, am intrigued to see this form of Vishnu."

(12.3) Shiva and Uma, accompanied by their followers, soon arrived in Svetadvipa. Vishnu personally greeted them, and after Shiva bowed at his feet, he affectionately raised him and led the couple to a comfortable seat.

When they were all sitting at ease, Vishnu said, "What can I do for you, my dear Shiva?"

(12.4-5) Smiling, Shiva replied, "My Lord, you are the supreme living force of all beings; you control us all. Everything visible and invisible comes from you, yet you are separate from it all and never contaminated by matter.

(12.6-8) "As your form is spiritual, great saintly persons worship you to become free of the influence of your illusory energy. Furthermore, you never lament about anything since you are eternal, full of bliss and knowledge. We gods come from and derive our powers from you. Indeed, all living beings derive whatever they possess from you. You alone are independent. As there is no difference between the gold in an ornament and a gold mine, there is no difference between you and the creation which comes from you. Since you are everything, you are celebrated as the Absolute Truth. Due to ignorance, conditioned souls fail to understand this and instead see the world in terms of dualities."

Vishnu smiled. "Thank you, my dear Shiva, but not everyone agrees. Many think Brahman is superior to me, while others believe pious work is the supreme principle. As you know, so many theories about the ultimate truth abound."

(12.9) Shiva shook his head sadly. "These different philosophers don't understand that whatever they attribute as being supreme is you. For example, you are the Brahman, and you are religious principles. You are also devotional service, for you are the independent Supreme Person. You have no equal or superior."

Vishnu's face assumed a grave look. "Many would argue with this."

(12.10-11) Shiva said, "I am celebrated as the best of the gods, but I cannot fully understand your greatness or how you manifest the creation. Nor can Lord Brahma and all the greatest sages, headed by Marichi, all of whom are in the mode of goodness. So what do these lesser philosophers know? They are either from the human or Asura races, so their natures are heavily contaminated by ignorance and passion. How can they appreciate the truth about you? You alone know everything since, like the air, you pervade everything, both the moving and non-moving."

Vishnu smiled. "I am delighted by your wisdom, dear Shiva. Please ask me for whatever you desire."

(12.12-13) Shiva replied, "My dear Lord, I have seen all your transcendental incarnations, but I missed your appearance as a beautiful young woman. I wish to see the form you manifested to captivate the Asuras and enable the gods to drink the nectar. Eager to see this form, we have hurried here."

(12.14-16) Shiva fell silent, sitting stoically with his trident in hand. He had heard Vishnu's Mohini incarnation had captivated everyone, but he would not be bewitched.[69] He was so advanced in yoga that not even Durga could enchant him.[70] Understanding Shiva's mind, Vishnu smiled. His pride would soon be curbed.

(12.17) Vishnu then vanished. Shiva and Uma stood up in surprise. Where had the Lord gone? They searched the palace but could not find him anywhere. Disappointed and bewildered by Vishnu's behaviour, they returned to Mount Kailasha accompanied by their followers.

(12.18-20) As they passed through a nearby forest of trees with reddish-pink leaves and carpeted with varieties of flowers, Shiva spotted a beautiful woman playing with a ball. Her hips were covered with a bright sari and ornamented with a sparkling belt. Her delicate waist seemed as if it might give way under the weight of her buxom breasts and heavy flower garland as she ran here and there on her soft reddish feet, bouncing the ball. Her lovely eyes darted about following the ball, and her two brilliant bluish earrings swung back and forth. Locks of raven black hair fell around her face, highlighting her exquisite charm.

(12.21-22) As she moved about, her sari loosened, and her hair scattered. She tried to bind her hair with a delicate hand while simultaneously bouncing the ball with her other hand. Shiva, his wife, and all his ghostly followers became mesmerised by her divine beauty. She saw Shiva watching her, and while continuing to play with her ball, she frequently glanced his way and smiled coyly. Catching her glance, Shiva felt his heart leap. The girl was attracted to him! He gazed at her, forgetting that his wife and followers were with him.

(12.23-25) Suddenly the ball slipped away from her, and as she hurried to catch it, her broad hips swaying, a breeze blew off her fine dress, which fell in a heap along with her belt. She stood naked before Shiva, who gulped and stared at her without blinking. Their eyes locked and he became consumed with desire for her. Believing the attraction was mutual, he ran toward her, careless of Uma's presence.

(12.26-30) The girl tried vainly to cover her nudity with her hands and glanced down bashfully. With a shy smile, she hid behind some trees. Wholly overcome by lust, Shiva ran after her like a lusty elephant pursuing its mate. Moving swiftly, he caught her by her braid and drew her to him. She pulled away and tried to resist Shiva's embrace, but to no

ENCHANTING PASTIMES

avail. Even though Shiva embraced her tightly, she managed to writhe free. Uma frowned as she saw her husband captivated by Mohini. Drawing a deep breath, she calmed her mind. It was hardly surprising. This was the Supreme Lord. Who would not be attracted?

(12.31-33) Meanwhile, Shiva, maddened by lust, chased Mohini like an elephant in rut chasing a she-elephant in her season. As he did so, he involuntarily discharged semen.

Uma was shocked. Shiva had previously never discharged semen other than to beget a child. She saw in wonder that wherever his semen fell, mines of gold and silver appeared.

(12.34) Shiva continued to chase Mohini as she fled to regions where great sages lived, such as riverbanks and lakesides, over mountains and through forests and gardens. Observing this, the sages said, "If even Lord Shiva can become mad after a woman, what then of us?" Each of them resolved to be ever more cautious to avoid association with the opposite sex.

(12.35-36) After fully discharging semen, Shiva came to his senses and stopped chasing Mohini. He shook his head. How had he become so deluded? Surely it was Lord Vishnu's supreme power that had overcome him. Only Vishnu could have bewildered him so. Shiva felt reassured. It was hardly surprising then that he had lost his senses. No one can excel Vishnu and to be defeated by him was not a fault.

(12.37-39) Seeing that Shiva had stopped chasing her and was now peaceful, the girl turned and faced him. She transformed into Vishnu, his four hands holding the conch, lotus, club and *chakra*. Smiling, he approached Shiva and said, "O best of gods, although you have been amply harassed because of seeing my incarnation as Mohini, the enchantress, I am happy to see that you are again self-composed. Let there be all good fortune for you. Due to their desire to enjoy independently of me, everyone in the material world, except for you, is prey to lust. Therefore, everyone is controlled by my material energy apart from yourself."

(12.40) Shiva's wife caught up to them as they spoke. Vishnu greeted her warmly. "Ah! Durga! Welcome!"

Turning back to Shiva, he said, "As you know, your wife cooperates with me in creating the material world by manifesting the three modes of nature. She allures everyone in the universe, but by my blessing, she will not be able to bewilder you."

(12.41) Shiva folded his palms and said, "O Supreme Personality of Godhead, who bears the mark of the goddess of fortune on your chest, I offer you my repeated obeisance."

He circumambulated Vishnu three times and, after receiving his permission, returned to Kailasha along with his associates.

(12.42-43) As they travelled home, Shiva jovially addressed his wife. "My dear Bhavani, although you are celebrated as the unborn Lord's illusory potency, surely you were as impressed as I by his power of illusion. If even I, one of his principal expansions, could be deluded by him, what to speak of those controlled by you."

They rode for a few minutes in silence, each marvelling over Vishnu's mastery over everyone.

(12.44) Shiva broke their reverie. "Do you remember when I performed mystic yoga for one thousand years, and afterwards, you asked me upon whom I was meditating?"

Durga replied, "Yes, I remember it well."

Shiva smiled. "I was meditating on this same Lord Vishnu. He is so great that he is not affected by time, which controls everything else, nor is he known by the Vedas, which know everything."

***

(12.45-46) Shukadeva glanced up at the moon. It was well into the third night of his continuous narration. Parikit still sat fully alert, his eyes fixed upon the sage. Owls hooted in the deep forest and night birds flapped across the river, which gleamed in the moonlight. He said, "My dear king, that person who bore Mount Meru on his back during the Milk Ocean's churning is no other than Krishna, who bears the Sharnga bow. Can you now better appreciate the Lord's great prowess? Whoever constantly hears this pastime will succeed in all his endeavours. Indeed, describing any of the Lord's glorious pastimes destroys all one's suffering."

(12.47) Shukadeva placed his palms together and bowed his head, saying, "I offer my respectful obeisance unto the Supreme Personality of Godhead, who, assuming the form of a beautiful woman, bewildered the Asuras and distributed to the gods the nectar produced from churning the Milk Ocean."

13
The Manus

Parikit was eager to hear more. "My lord, please tell me of the Lord's incarnations during the reign of other Manus."[71]

(13.1-6) "My dear king," Shukadeva said, "the current Manu in whose reign we live is the seventh, Shraddhadeva. He is the sun god Vivasvan's son and is therefore known as Vaivasvata Manu."

Shukadeva explained who filled the post of Indra, the other gods, and seven primary sages during Shraddhadeva's rule. He concluded by describing how Krishna would appear as the dwarf Vamana, the youngest son of Kashyapa and Aditi.

(13.7-12) Having described all the Manus who had already appeared, Shukadeva went on to give the names of the seven Manus who would appear in the future, along with details about who would accept the post of Indra, the other gods, and the seven sages during their reigns, as well as details about the Lord's incarnation in those eras. (Appendix A) He gave special attention to describing the dynasty of Savarni, the eighth Manu and significant events in his reign. (Appendix B) "During Savarni's reign, King Bali will become Indra."

Parikit looked surprised. "Do you mean Bali, the son of Virochana?"

"Yes."

"Is he not one of the Asuras?"

(13.13-14) "Yes. When he gifted Lord Vishnu three paces of land in charity, the Lord used that opportunity to take everything from him. However, Bali's response very much pleased Vishnu. Consequently, Bali achieved spiritual perfection. Though at first Vishnu bound Bali with ropes, later he affectionately installed him as the king of Sutala, which is more opulent than the heavenly planets. King Bali lives there and is more comfortably situated than even Indra."

(13.15-16) He then told Parikit other details about Savarni Manu's reign. "You will be interested to know that some of those who will become the seven sages under Savarni Manu are associated with your dynasty. They are Galava, Diptiman, Parashurama, Ashvatthama, Kripacharya, Rishyashringa, and my father, Vyasadeva."

Parikit became absorbed in thought, remembering these personalities. Galava was one of the many sages who came to Hastinapura to see Krishna and Balarama.[72] Diptiman was one of Krishna's sons.[73] Parashurama was the famous son of Jamadagni, who had practically obliterated the warrior class by defeating them in twenty-one battles.[74] Ashvatthama, the son of Drona, had tried to kill him while he was still an unborn baby.[75] Kripacharya later became their trusted advisor despite having fought against the Pandavas.[76] Rishyashringa was the sage born with deerlike horns growing from his forehead.[77] He was famous for having been instrumental in the appearance of Lord Rama and his three illustrious brothers.[78]

(13.17-35) Shukadeva added that in that era, Krishna's incarnation, Sarvabhauma, would depose Purandara from his post as Indra and install Bali as the king of heaven. He summarised the reign of the remaining six Manus, mentioning who Indra and the other administrative gods would be in those eras. He also named the seven sages and the Vishnu incarnation associated with each Manu.

(13.36) Finally, he said, "I have described fourteen Manus appearing in the past, present and future. Their total duration is one thousand *yuga* cycles or one day of Brahma. This is called a *kalpa*."

14
The Cosmic Administration

(14.1) Parikit was fascinated to learn that in the era of each Manu, the universal administration changed. He said, "O great sage, kindly describe the duties of the Manus and their administrations. I am also curious to know how they are appointed to these positions.

(14.2-3) Shukadeva replied, "Do you remember I told you the Supreme Lord, Yagya became the Indra during Svayambhuva Manu's reign?"[79]

"Yes, master."

"Well, in each era, the Vishnu incarnations such as Yagya appoint and oversee the Manus, the administrative gods, and the seven sages."

Shukadeva explained that the universe goes through cycles of four ages: Satya, Treta, Dvapara and Kali *yugas*. In Satya-yuga, the religious principles are observed in full, without deviation. In Treta-yuga, these principles are somewhat neglected, and only three-fourths of the religious duties continue. In Dvapara-yuga, only half remain; in Kali-yuga, only a fourth remain, and even they gradually disappear. By the end of Kali-yuga, virtually all religious principles are lost, and people become highly degraded.

(14.4-7) "At the end of Kali-yuga, it is the duty of the seven sages[80] to re-establish service to Krishna as the eternal religious principle in human society. Then the Lord instructs the Manus to re-establish the religious duties associated with the four occupations: brahmins, *kshatriyas*, *vaishyas*, and *shudras*. Their sons and grandson are responsible for protecting religious principles throughout each era. In return, they enjoy the results of sacrifices performed on earth along with the administrative gods. Indra, who enjoys great opulence by Vishnu's grace, is responsible for maintaining all creatures by providing rain to all the planets throughout the universe.

(14.8-9) "In each age, Krishna advents as liberated souls, such as the four Kumaras, to teach transcendental knowledge. He assumes the form of great sages like Yagyavalkya to teach the principles by which people can live piously, and he takes the form of great yogis like Dattatreya to teach the mystic yoga system. As the Prajapatis like Marichi, the Lord generates progeny, and as the kingly descendants of Manu, he kills thieves and other criminals.[81] In the form of time, Krishna destroys everything. As the qualities of these leaders of human society come from Krishna, all material attributes come from him, including conventionally unpleasant ones like fatness and thinness, aging and senility."[82]

Parikit said, "So the Lord causes all actions and reactions in the material universe."

(14.10) "Yes, exactly," replied Shukadeva. "So many philosophers try to understand the ultimate cause behind everything, but because they are deluded by the Lord's illusory energy, despite all their research and wrangling, they cannot see the cause is Vishnu, and even if they do accept that, they cannot understand his acts or why he performs them."[83]

Parikit sighed. "I guess it's best to stop worrying about things then, and just be happy chanting Krishna's glories."

(14.11) Shukadeva laughed. "I have now finished explaining how each of Brahma's days is divided into fourteen eras, each presided over by a different Manu."

15
The Great King Bali

Parikit became pensive. He could not help his desire to at least try to understand Krishna's pastimes.

"What is on your mind?" asked Shukadeva.

(15.1-2) "Earlier, you said Vamana asked Bali to give him three paces of land in charity, but after receiving the gift, he arrested Bali. I cannot understand why he did that. Furthermore, since the Lord is the proprietor of everything, why did he beg for charity like a poor man? If possible, please explain the mystery of these contradictions to me."

"Ah! Excellent questions," said Shukadeva. "Do you remember I told you how Bali was mortally wounded in the battle with the gods?"

"Yes, that happened after Mohini tricked the Asuras into letting her give the gods the nectar."

"That's right! Now hear what happened next."

***

(15.3-4) Bedraggled and beaten, the surviving Asuras slowly returned to the battlefield and, as ordered by Narada, gathered the bodies of the dead and wounded, including that of Bali. They piled the bodies in their chariots and took them to Mount Astagiri.[84] There, to their great relief, they found Shukra's hermitage, just as Narada had said they would.

Falling flat before Shukra, they made their obeisances. Then rising to their knees, they said, "O powerful descendant of Sage Bhrigu,[85] we take shelter of you. Please revive our comrades."

Shukra had the bodies laid out before him. He entered a deep trance, quietly intoning the Sanjivani mantras. After some minutes, the slain and wounded warriors, including Bali, sat up as if waking from slumber. When he was told what had happened, Bali bowed before Shukra.

"My lord," he said, "I am your humble servant."

Bali attended to Shukra day and night, satisfying his every need. Within his heart, the Daitya king thought continuously of Indra. The weak and cowardly god had only defeated him thanks to Vishnu's intervention. He looked across at Shukra, who sat in silent meditation under a tree. Surely that powerful sage could help him gain revenge. Like Vishnu, he, too, could raise men from the dead. If anyone could find a way to overcome the gods, it would be Shukra. Bali resolved to serve him even more assiduously.

The powerful mystic, Shukra, was aware of his disciple's thoughts, and he was gratified by his faith in and devotion to him. That afternoon, as Bali served his meal, Shukra smiled at him affectionately and said, "You have served me for many months, Bali. I am most pleased with you. Ask me for a boon."

Bali bowed his head and meekly replied, "Continual service to your exalted self is the only boon I seek."

Shukra smiled and said, "That is the right sentiment for a disciple, but I know the desire that burns your heart day and night. You wish to conquer Indra."

Bali looked at his master in awe. Shukra was truly a great mystic who could understand the hearts of all beings.

Shukra continued, "Tomorrow at dawn, you should take a ritual bath, purifying yourself completely. Then, along with other brahmin descendants of my illustrious ancestor, Bhrigu, I shall engage you in performing the powerful fire sacrifice known as the Vishvajit."

(15.5-6) The following day, having bathed and dressed, Bali sat in front of his guru in the sacrificial arena. When Shukra poured the last libation of ghee into the fire, there appeared a celestial chariot covered with gold and silk, bearing a flag marked with a lion and drawn by yellow horses like those of Indra. Within the chariot lay a gilded bow, two quivers of infallible arrows, and celestial armour. His grandfather, Prahlada, placed an unfading garland of flowers around his neck, and Shukra gave him a conch.

(15.7-9) Bali first circumambulated the brahmins headed by Shukra and made his obeisance. He then saluted his grandfather and bowed to him. Two of his chief generals stepped forward and assisted Bali in donning the impenetrable golden armour. Decked with the divine garland, with a jewelled sword hanging from his hips and a quiver of gold fletched arrows slung over his shoulders, holding his bow and conch shell, his arms decorated with golden bangles and his ears with sapphire earrings, he alighted the chariot, shining like a sacred fire. A great uproar arose as the assembled Daitya soldiers repeatedly called out, "Victory to King Bali!"

(15.10-11) The next day Bali met outside his palace with the Daitya chiefs, all equal to him in strength, opulence and beauty. Each was tall and muscular, and when they assembled with the Daitya soldiers, it seemed they could burn all directions by their mere glance.

Bali delegated each general with different preparations for the battle against the gods. Then raising both arms, he declared, "We march against Indra's capital one week from today!" Hearing this, the Asuras sent up a tremendous roar.

On the designated day of departure, it seemed like an ocean of chariots, and ferocious animals with fierce warriors mounted on their backs had assembled outside the Daitya city. Their tall gleaming spears swaying about were like its glistening waves, and the roar of the jubilant soldiers sounded like the crashing of surf on the seashore. As the army began its march, the ground trembled, and terrified creatures fled in all directions.

(15.12-13) Meanwhile, in Amaravati, the gods were strolling in the beautiful orchards and woods, amongst which was the famous Nandana garden. It was spring, and the trees, heavy with fruits and flowers, were bent low. The chirping birds and buzzing bees further enhanced the charming atmosphere. Many lotus ponds full of swans, cranes, *chakravakas*, and ducks were dotted throughout the gardens, and beautiful women could be seen playing with abandon, confident that protected by the gods, they had nothing to fear.

(15.14-16) The gods felt assured that their city was impenetrable. It was surrounded by trenches full of Ganges water and a high wall that looked like a great ring of fire. Along the top of the wall were many parapets from which soldiers could repel any enemy. The city had been constructed by Vishvakarma and could only be accessed through solid iron doors embedded with gold plates, and gates made of excellent marble. It abounded with delightful public squares, wide tree-lined avenues, leisure palaces, pearl-inlaid arches, and ornate seats of diamond and coral. Not less than one hundred million aircraft carried the celestials here and there.

(15.17-18) Amaravati was further beautified by the numerous enchanting ever-youthful women who loitered here and there, glittering like sparkling fires in their attractive outfits. These women, all sporting prominent busts, were known as Shyama because their bodies were warm in the winter and cool in the summer. The fragrance from the flowers in their hair wafted everywhere.

(15.19) Many Apsara women also sauntered along Amaravati's streets, always filled with the fragrant white smoke of *aguru* incense emanating from the mansions lining the streets, whose windows were decorated with golden filigree.

(15.20-21) The city was shaded by canopies decorated with pearls, and the palace domes had flags bordered with gold and pearls. Amaravati constantly resounded with the vibrations of peacocks, pigeons and bees, and above the city flew aeroplanes full of beautiful women who constantly chanted auspicious songs pleasing to the ear. The sounds of *mridangas*, conch shells, kettledrums, flutes and well-tuned stringed instruments playing in concert floated through the air, and Gandharvas danced and sang throughout the city. All these features of Amaravati made the celestials feel that their city was more beautiful than beauty itself.

(15.22) Despite the unrivalled opulence and facility for sensual enjoyment, no one in Amaravati was sinful, envious, cunning, falsely proud, lusty, greedy, or violent toward other living entities, and the celestials were sure that no immoral person could ever again enter their city.

(15.23) Thus it was that under cover of night, as the complacent gods slept in the embrace of their wives, Bali gathered his forces outside Amaravati. They worked quickly and quietly, building bridges over the moat and setting up great catapults to hurl huge blazing boulders far over the wall. As the first light of day appeared, Bali's numberless soldiers were positioned all around the high wall, and his archers were strategically placed to counter any defence from the guards. Bali then blew a terrific blast on his mighty conch shell to signal the start of the assault on the city. The intolerable roar of that conch, given to Bali by Shukra, awoke the heavenly damsels who sat up in fear. Indra and the other gods raced from their palaces, pulling on their armour. They pushed through the pandemonium on the streets of Amaravati toward the city walls. Women could be heard screaming in terror as the Asuras' missiles landed on their homes, setting them alight.

(15.24) Indra ascended a watchtower and looked at the sea of warriors that stretched in all directions. In their midst Bali shone like the sun. Indra said to his aide, "Bali has spared no effort. It seems he is intent on capturing Amaravati. Let us go quickly and consult Brihaspati."

The sage resided in a secluded coppice in the heart of Amaravati. When Indra, accompanied by the principal gods, arrived there, Brihaspati was seated before the sacrificial fire worshipping Vishnu.

(15.25-26) "My lord," Indra called out. "Our old enemy Bali is alive. Even as we speak, his soldiers are penetrating our defences. Somehow, he has obtained such astonishing power that I fear we will be unable to resist his assault. Indeed, I do not think anyone can counter his forces. He looks like the annihilating *samvartaka* fire. He will swallow the entire universe, lick up the ten directions, and set everywhere ablaze by his glance.

(15.27) Brihaspati listened with concern. Indra folded his palms and said, "O all-seeing sage, what is the reason for Bali's newfound strength, endeavour, influence and invincibility? How has he become so powerful?"

(15.28) Brihaspati closed his eyes in meditation. On opening them, he replied, "Hear me, O king of the gods. Bhrigu's brahmin descendants, pleased with their disciple Bali, have endowed him with extraordinary power."

Indra fell to the ground with his hands clasped in prayer, "My lord and master, please tell me how I might defeat him."

(15.29) Brihaspati slowly shook his head, "Neither you nor your men can now conquer Bali. Indeed, none but the Lord can defeat him, for he is equipped with the brahmins' supreme spiritual power. As no one can stand before Yamaraja, no one can now stand before King Bali."

Indra stared at his preceptor, his eyes wide open in panic. "What should I do?"

(15.30) Placing a hand on Indra's shoulder, Brihaspati urged him to leave Amaravati immediately and go into hiding along with the other gods.

Tears sprung to the gods' eyes, and they looked forlornly at one another. Was this indeed the end for them? Were they destined to live the rest of their lives exiled from their beloved Amaravati?

(15.31) Understanding their fear, Brihaspati consoled them, "At present, Bali is invincible because of the brahmins' benediction, but later, when he insults them, he will be vanquished along with his friends and accomplices."

Dawn had fully broken, and the victory cries of the Asura soldiers resounded as they forced open the city's gates. Brihaspati urged Indra, "You have no time to waste. Leave at once!"

(15.32) The swans, cranes, *chakravakas* and ducks in the numerous parks in Amaravati were swarming the skies, panicked by the din. By their mystic powers, the gods transformed themselves into these different species of birds and merged in among the terrified flocks leaving the city.

(15.33) Bali sat regally in his chariot, surrounded by his generals, and rode down Amaravati's wide central avenue. The city's brahmins, headed by Brihaspati, greeted Bali with a ritual reception and flower garlands.

"O King Bali," Brihaspati said, "I welcome you, the celebrated Prahlada's grandson and the dear disciple of the powerful Shukra. As befitting your great heritage, grant your protection to the women and citizens of Amaravati. Let not your men torment them."

Turning to his generals, who flanked him on either side, Bali proclaimed, "Death shall be the lot of anyone who harasses those who have sought my protection. Declare this to every man in my army."

Bali and the Daityas then assumed the rule of the universe. Bali brought his spiritual master Shukra to Amaravati, and along with his disciples, the Daitya preceptor resided in a hermitage close to Bali's palace. Bali went daily to worship and serve Shukra for several hours.

One morning, as Bali massaged his spiritual master's legs, Shukra said, "Bali, I am most pleased with you. You are truly a noble soul and an ideal disciple."

The sage was enjoying his new status as the guru of the lord of the universe. He raised a hand in blessing and said, "May your opulence continue to increase."

Bali humbly bowed, "I am ever your servant, my lord. My only desire in life is to satisfy you."

(15.34) Shukra smiled and said, "And I desire to see your continued prosperity. I have been considering how you can strengthen your position. Indra had to perform one hundred horse sacrifices to secure his standing as the king of heaven. You should now do the same."

(15.35-36) Bali immediately started to make the arrangements, and under the careful guidance of Shukra, he completed a hundred sacrifices. As a result of this, his reputation spread throughout the three worlds. He shone like the brilliant moon in a clear sky. Favoured by Shukra, Bali felt unassailable in his position as the undisputed ruler of the universe.

16
Sage Kashyapa Instructs Aditi

(16.1) After the gods fled into hiding, their mother, Aditi, became morose. She spent her time alone in her darkened room, thinking of her powerful husband, Kashyapa. When would he return? The sage had been away for some time, performing his austerities and meditation high up on Mount Mandara. She remembered when she had practised much penance with her husband with the desire for good progeny. In due course, she had brought forth the gods. Thinking of their present condition pained her heart. The beautiful palace and many servants Kashyapa had left her with could not assuage her sorrow. With neither her husband nor sons with her, she felt vulnerable and unprotected.

Aditi rose from her couch and moved to the latticed window. Drawing back the heavy silk curtain, she looked at her celestial surroundings. Blossoming trees whose branches laden with ripened fruits hung down to the ground. Perfectly manicured gardens with twisting paths lined with beds of multi-coloured flowers. Swans and ducks playing in clear ponds among clusters of lotuses and lilies.

(16.2-3) The goddess felt no happiness observing this heavenly scene. She was about to turn away from the window when she saw her ascetic husband approaching. He strode toward the palace, clad in deerskin and carrying only his water pot and staff. As the sage came up the path, he was surprised to see no festoons of flags and flower garlands nor hear the usual sounds of festivity in Aditi's home. When he passed through the golden gates, the servants greeted him sombrely. Usually, they would be cheerful and dash to tell Aditi of his arrival.

Anxious at heart, the sage entered his wife's quarters, where he found her sitting alone, her clothes and hair unkempt, and her face tear-stained and shrivelled. Kashyapa was shocked. He had never seen Aditi in such a condition. The goddess normally kept herself immaculately groomed. Her face would shine with natural beauty and elegance.

Seeing her husband enter, Aditi quickly rose to greet him. She offered her obeisance and welcomed him with gentle speech. Then she led him to a raised seat, washed his feet with warm water, and dried them with a soft cloth. Bringing him a pitcher of cool water to quench his thirst, she served him a meal. Kashyapa watched her with a look of concern on his face but said nothing, waiting until she finished serving him. Finally, when the meal was complete and the servants had cleared away the remnants, she came and sat near her husband with downcast eyes.

(16.4) Kashyapa took Aditi's hand in his own. "Gentle lady, why are you so unhappy? Has there been any irregularity regarding religious principles? Have the brahmins or people in general erred from their duties?"

(16.5-7) Aditi shook her head but kept her eyes down, wringing her hands. Kashyapa reached over and tenderly raised her face. Looking into her tear-filled eyes, he said, "As a woman, it is natural that you are attached to having a comfortable and happy home. However, if you also properly follow the duties of household life, your activities will elevate you to transcendence. Has there been any discrepancy in your religious practice? Did you at any time neglect a guest, even one uninvited? For a dutiful householder, this is always a grave omission."

"Yes, my lord. I understand all this."

(16.8-9) Kashyapa considered what other inauspicious act could have brought such unhappiness into his home. "O chaste lady, when I left home, were you so disturbed that you failed to offer oblations of ghee into the sacrificial fire? You, of course, know that Vishnu is worshipped by such oblations and by feeding brahmins. Only by satisfying Vishnu can one live on the higher planets, for he is the very soul of the gods."

Aditi again indicated that she understood.

(16.10) Kashyapa frowned. What could have made Aditi so distraught? Slowly it dawned on him what the problem might be. "O great-minded lady, are all your sons faring well? I can see you are troubled. Pray tell me why."

(16.11-13) Aditi wiped her tears away. "Respected saintly husband, everything is well with the brahmins, cows, my religious principles, and the welfare of people in general. I always carefully perform my religious duties; therefore, I enjoy prosperity, and my bodily needs are met. Beloved husband, since I always remember your instructions, there is no possibility that I would neglect to offer oblations to the sacrificial fire, or to take proper care of guests, servants, or beggars. My lord, I am confident my desires can be fulfilled since you, a great Prajapati, personally guide me in my religious duties."

The goddess hesitated to say more. After all, her husband was the father of not only her sons but also the Asuras. Would he favour her sons over those of Diti, her sister and co-wife?

Kashyapa waited expectantly.

(16.14-16) "O son of Marichi," Aditi continued, "both the gods and Asuras come from you; therefore, like Lord Vishnu, you are equal toward them both. Yet even though Vishnu is equal to all, he especially supports the devotees. Therefore, my lord, please favour your maidservant. My sons have been deprived of their opulence by the Daityas.[86] Indeed, they have been exiled and are drowning in an ocean of grief. Kindly give them protection."

(16.17) Tears streamed down Aditi's face, and her voice choked. Taking hold of her husband's hands and pressing them to her heart, she pleaded, "O best of sages, best of those who grant auspicious benedictions, please consider my situation and bestow upon my sons blessings by which they can regain what they have lost."

Kashyapa sighed. There was always conflict between the sons of Aditi and Diti. One or other of them was always unhappy, asking for his help to favour her sons over the sons of the other. Still, it was his duty as their husband to elevate them spiritually.

(16.18) Kashyapa said, "Alas, how powerful is Vishnu's illusory energy by which the entire world is bound by affection for children."

Aditi looked quizzically at her husband. Was he denying her request or acquiescing?

(16.19) Seeing her puzzlement, Kashyapa explained. "Dear Aditi, why do you worry about your sons' material bodies? The eternal spirit soul is different from the body it inhabits. Only because of bodily attachment do we regard someone as our relative. These illusory relationships are based upon misunderstanding."

Tears fell from Aditi's large and beautiful eyes. Her husband was right, but her heart ached for her sons. If Kashyapa would not help them, then what was she to do?

Kashyapa was disinclined to side with either party against the other. Nevertheless, he would instruct Aditi in a manner that would purify her consciousness, as he had previously done for Diti when he told her about the Pumsavana ritual.[87]

The sage said, "Aditi, do not cry. I will tell you what you can do for your sons."

Aditi looked up at him, smiling. "Thank you, my lord!"

(16.20-21) "My dear goddess," began Kashyapa as his wife sat before him attentively. "Engage in devotional service to the Supreme Person, the master of everything, who can subdue all enemies, and who sits within everyone's heart. Only that all-powerful person, Krishna, can bestow auspicious benedictions upon everyone, for he is the master of the universe. The Lord is always merciful to the poor. If you serve him with love, he will surely fulfil your desires. Any method other than devotional service will prove useless. That is my opinion."

(16.22-23) Eager to begin her worship immediately, the pious Aditi asked, "Great brahmin, tell me the regulative principles by which I may worship the Lord so he will be pleased with me and fulfil my desires. Please teach me everything I need to do so that Krishna will save my sons and me."

(16.24) Kashyapa replied, "When I desired offspring, I questioned Lord Brahma. I shall explain to you the process he instructed me, by which Krishna is satisfied."

(16.25) Kashyapa described the ritual known as Payovrata, the 'milk vow', which entailed subsisting only on milk and worshipping Krishna with devotion. "Very soon, the bright fortnight spanning February and March will arrive. Start your vow at the beginning of this period until the day after the next Ekadasi day."

(16.26-27) He taught her how to take a ritual bath and recite a prayer to the earth goddess. "O mother earth! Lord Varaha raised you from the bottom of the universe and gave you a place to stay. I pray that you kindly vanquish all the reactions of my sinful life. I offer you my respectful obeisance."

(16.28-30) Kashyapa explained that daily she should worship Krishna in the form of his deity, as well as in the sun, water, fire and the spiritual master while praying, "O Lord, greatest of all, you are the Supersoul in everyone's heart and the witness of everything. You are famous as Vasudeva because you are the supreme all-pervading person. I offer you my respectful obeisance. You are invisible to material eyes, but you know everything and teach the Sankhya system by which reality can be understood.

(16.31-35) "I offer my respectful obeisance to you who bestows the results of sacrifice and are famed as the Lord with two heads, three legs, four horns and seven hands."[88] I offer obeisance to your incarnations such as Shiva, Brahma,[89] Nara-Narayana Rishi, and to the Lord of the Goddess of Fortune, Keshava, who dresses in yellow garments and has a dark blue complexion.[90]

(16.36-37) "O most exalted and venerable Lord, best of those who bestow benediction, you can fulfil everyone's desire, and therefore the wise worship you for their welfare. All the gods and the goddess of fortune adore the fragrance of your lotus feet. May you be pleased with me."

(16.38-42) Kashyapa told Aditi that after receiving Vishnu with this prayer, she should offer him water to wash his feet, hands and mouth. She should present him flower garlands, incense and other items while chanting the twelve-syllable mantra, '*om namo bhagavata vasudevaya*'. "If sufficient milk is available, offer the deity sweet rice with ghee and molasses while continuing to chant. You should also offer some into the fire. After the offering is complete, give the *prasadam* to a Vaishnava. You may also take some. Next, offer the deity water for washing his hands and mouth, and then proffer cut betel nut. Conclude your worship by quietly chanting the same mantra one hundred and eight times, circling the deity, and then offering your prostrated obeisance."

"What should I do with the flowers, incense etc., which I offered Krishna?" asked Aditi.

(16.43-45) "Touch them to your head, then throw them in a sacred place. You should distribute the leftover rice pudding to at least two brahmins. When they are satisfied, ask their permission before taking your meal along with your friends or family. In the morning, bathe and repeat the same worship as the day before. Throughout this period, you should observe strict celibacy.

(16.46-49) "You should worship the Lord like this with great faith and devotion for twelve days, during which time you should only eat the sweet rice pudding. Remember to offer oblations daily into the fire and feed the brahmins. Continue the same worship for the following fortnight while maintaining celibacy. You should also sleep on the floor, bathe three times a day, avoid all frivolous talk, and eschew all envy and violence toward any living entity.

(16.50-54) "On the final day of the second fortnight, guided by learned brahmins, bathe the deity with milk, yoghurt, ghee, sugar and honey. Spend lavishly for the Lord's worship. As well as offering him sweet rice, prepare many other varieties of foodstuff. While offering him everything, recite the Purusha-shukta mantra. Be sure to satisfy the chief priest and his assistants with gifts of cloth, ornaments and cows. This concludes Krishna's worship. O most auspicious lady, as well as satisfying the priests, be attentive to satisfy all the other brahmins and guests present."

"Should I give the same gifts to everyone?"

(16.55-56) "That's not required. Just give the chief priest and his assistants the gifts I mentioned, plus some monetary contribution. To everyone else, distribute ample *prasadam*. Make sure the poor, the blind, the non-devotees, and those who are not brahmins, even the lowest classes, all receive Krishna's *prasadam*. This will very much please Krishna. Once everyone is fed to their satisfaction, you may eat along with your friends and family."

"Is there anything else I need to do?"

(16.57-58) "Yes, every day throughout your month-long vow, while the Lord's worship is being performed, also make sure his praises are sung in accompaniment with musical instruments and dancing, followed by the recitation of the *Srimad Bhagavatam*. By following this vow, known as *payovrata*, you will satisfy Krishna. My grandfather,

Brahma, taught me this exactly as I am now instructing you."

(16.59-62) After concluding his detailed instructions, Kashyapa further encouraged his beloved wife. "Most fortunate lady, with confidence, execute this great vow exactly as I have explained it to you. By this sacrifice, the best of all ritualistic ceremonies, one automatically derives the benefit of all others. It includes the highest austerity, charity, and sacrifice, for it pleases Krishna. Indeed, it is the best means for satisfying the Supreme Person. If you follow it carefully, strictly observing the regulative principles, the Lord will be quickly pleased with you and will fulfil your desires."

17
Aditi sees Lord Vishnu

(17.1-3) When Kashyapa finished his instructions, Aditi immediately implemented them to the best of her ability. Her mind and senses constantly tried to allure her to other things, but as an expert equestrian trains wild horses, she controlled her mind and kept it fixed on performing the Payovrata for Krishna's pleasure.

(17.4-5) After her vow was complete, Vishnu appeared before her dressed in yellow garments, bearing a conch shell, disc, club and lotus in his four graceful hands. Aditi gazed unblinkingly at him in rapturous wonder. She began to horripilate with transcendental bliss. Her body trembled, and tears of ecstatic love streamed down her face. She rose and then fell to the ground like a rod in respectful obeisance.

(17.6-7) Finally, Aditi raised herself and stood with folded hands before Vishnu, desiring to offer him prayers of welcome. Her eyes drank in his transcendental beauty, and her mind raced excitedly. Here was the Supreme Lord himself, the husband of the goddess of fortune and the master of the universe. If pleased with her sacrifice, he would surely restore her sons' wealth and deliver the world from the hands of the Asuras.[91]

(17.8) In a trembling voice, Aditi said, "O master and enjoyer of all sacrificial ceremonies, you are infallible and famous everywhere. Just chanting your holy name spreads good fortune to all. You are the supreme personality and controller. Everywhere connected with you becomes a place of pilgrimage. You protect the poor, suffering living entities, and now you have appeared to diminish our misery. Please bestow good fortune on us.

(17.9-10) "You engage your material energy to create, maintain and annihilate the universe, but you are never affected by this energy. You are always in transcendence, never affected by illusion. Thus, your guidance is infallible and always appropriate. Please accept my respectful obeisance. O unlimitedly powerful Lord, by your grace, one can very easily achieve a lifetime like Brahma's, residence in any planetary system one desires, as well as all wealth, opulence and mystic power. What then of the small accomplishment of defeating one's enemies?"

(17.11-16) Aditi gazed at Vishnu, the Supersoul in every heart, whose lotus-petal eyes looked affectionately at her. He said, "O mother of the gods, I know of your long-cherished desires for your sons' welfare. They have been driven from the heavens by their enemies, and you wish me to retrieve their kingdom and kill their enemies. You want your sons to again live in the heavens, having regained their lost reputation and opulence. However, I think the Asuras cannot yet be conquered in battle, for the brahmins protect them. Since brahmins are dear to me, not even I interfere with someone they protect. Therefore, the use of force against them will not succeed."

Aditi's face fell in disappointment. Had her austerities been in vain?

(17.17) Vishnu spoke reassuringly, "Do not be distressed, dear lady. I am most satisfied by your Payovrata vow and will find a way to favour you. Worship of me never goes in vain but certainly gives the desired result according to what one deserves."

Wiping away her tears, Aditi looked at Vishnu with a puzzled expression. What did he have in mind? How could the Asuras be defeated without a fight?

(17.18) Vishnu continued, "You have prayed to me and properly worshipped me. I am also pleased with your husband's asceticism. Therefore, I shall become your son and protect your other sons."

Aditi's heart leapt. The Lord would become her son! How wonderful.

(17.19-20) "Now, dear lady, since your husband has been purified by his austerity, worship him, knowing me to be situated in his body. However, do not reveal this to anyone, even if they ask. A confidential undertaking should never be divulged, or it will fail."

(17.21) With these words, Vishnu disappeared. Aditi's joy knew no bounds. The Lord had promised to save her sons, and his word was infallible. With great devotion, she approached her husband.

(17.22-23) Meanwhile, Kashyapa, seated in meditation, saw Krishna's expansion enter him. That night, by union with Aditi, he transferred the divine presence into her womb.[92] Over the coming months, the atmosphere of Kashyapa's home became increasingly auspicious. Aditi glowed with radiant beauty. However, she harboured doubt. How could sexual intercourse conceive the supreme transcendent Lord? When she placed her confusion before her husband, he said, "The Lord's appearance has nothing to do with the secretions during sexual intercourse."

"It seems like it."

"Do not misunderstand. Just as the wind creates friction between two pieces of wood, it appears like the wind and wood created the fire. However, fire is neither wind nor wood."[93]

(17.24) The omniscient Brahma could immediately understand the nature of Aditi's pregnancy. Unseen even by Aditi, he came daily to Kashyapa's ashram to chant Krishna's names and recite beautiful prayers to her unborn child.

(17.25-28) "All glories to the Supreme Person," he prayed. "Everyone glorifies your uncommon pastimes. Please accept my respectful obeisance, for you control the three modes of nature and are also the Lord of the transcendentalists. You pervade everything and enter the cores of everyone's hearts, yet the three planetary systems rest in your navel. Simultaneously, you are transcendental to the material universes. You formerly appeared as Prishni's son.[94] O supreme creator, you can only be understood from the Vedic statements, which celebrate you as the reservoir of unlimited potencies and the beginning, middle, and end of the material universes. You are the supreme time factor which carries everything in the cosmos as a deep flowing river carries branches and leaves which fall into it. Some say the living entities come from the original progenitors, but you are the origin of all beings. As a boat is the only hope for a drowning man, you are the only hope for the gods who have lost everything."

18
The Divine Dwarf

(18.1-6) When the astrological constellations were favourable at noon on the twelfth day of the waxing moon, Aditi gave birth to her divine son just as Brahma finished offering his prayers. Appearing in his four-armed Vishnu form, he was dressed in yellow garments, and his eyes seemed like the petals of a blooming lotus. Shark-shaped earrings swung by his cheeks, the brilliant Kaustubha gem hung around his neck, and his arms were adorned with sparkling golden bangles. A gorgeous flower garland decorated his chest, surrounded by black bees. He held a conch shell, club, lotus and disc in his four graceful hands. Vishnu's natural effulgence radiated everywhere, creating a pleasing atmosphere, and all living beings felt joyful.

(18.7-10) The sounds of conch shells, kettledrums, and other instruments reverberated loudly from all directions. Apsaras danced jubilantly while the Gandharvas sang. Great sages, the gods, the Manus, the Pitas and fire-gods appeared in the heavens to offer prayers. The Siddhas, Vidyadharas and other celestials gathered above Aditi's residence and showered it with flowers while dancing and singing Krishna's praises.

(18.11-12) Like a theatrical performer, Vishnu transformed his original form before his parents' eyes into that of a dwarf brahmin boy dressed as a *brahmachari*. Aditi was wonderstruck, and Kashyapa repeatedly called out in jubilation, "Jaya! Jaya!"

(18.13-14) The sages were delighted to see Vishnu appearing as a dwarf. "Look! He has come as Vamana!"[95] They then set about assisting Kashyapa in performing the *samskara* rituals beginning with the birth ceremony, then the hair-cutting ritual, and finally the initiation ceremony, giving Vamana his sacred thread.[96] During this ceremony, the sun god personally uttered the Gayatri mantra while Brihaspati offered Vamana his sacred thread. Kashyapa presented his son with a straw belt.

(18.15-17) The other celestials then came forward with their gifts for the child. Mother Earth offered him a deerskin; the moon god gave him the rod a brahmachari customarily carried; his mother, Aditi, gave him a cloth to wear as underwear, and Indra gave him an umbrella. Brahma presented Vamana with a waterpot; the seven sages gave him *kusha* grass, and Sarasvati gave him a string of *rudraksha* beads. Kuvera gave him a pot for begging alms and Shiva's wife, Bhagavati, gave him his first alms.

(18.18-19) Everyone present was dazzled by the Lord's effulgence. One god whispered, "Just see how his beauty surpasses all others!" Vamana then kindled a sacrificial fire and performed his first fire sacrifice.

(18.20) Finally, Brahma said, "My dear Lord, even as we speak, the powerful Bali is performing the Ashvamedha sacrifice under the direction of brahmins in Bhrigu's dynasty."

Vamana smiled and, rising from his own fire sacrifice, proceeded to Bali's. With his every step, the earth seemed to move.

One god exclaimed to his friends, "Just imagine his power. With his every step, he creates deep imprints in the surface of the earth!"

(18.21-22) Meanwhile, in the field known as Bhrigukaccha, on the northern bank of the Narmada River, brahmins were busy performing a fire sacrifice to increase Bali's influence and opulence. To their surprise, they became blinded by a brilliant effulgence, making it hard for them to see Bali or each other.

"What is this light?" one exclaimed. "It seems like the sun has risen in our very midst!"

"The sun god must have arrived," said another.

"How has the sun god dared to return?" snapped Shukra. "Does he not fear Bali's might?"

An assistant priest, examining the newcomer more carefully, said, "I don't think it is the sun-god, holy one. Possibly it is Agni, the fire god, coming to surrender to our king. Perhaps he desires to serve him during the sacrifice personally."

Shukra's son, Amarka, said, "I doubt any gods would dare come before King Bali. This must surely be the illustrious sage, Sanat Kumara, who has come to bless him."

(18.23) While the brahmins and their disciples discussed the possible identity of the newcomer, Vamana strolled into the sacrificial arena, holding his *brahmachari* rod, umbrella, and filled waterpot.

(18.25-28) Other than for his personal effulgence, he appeared like any other brahmin boy with a straw belt, a sacred thread, an upper deerskin garment, and matted locks of hair. Awed by the boy's beauty, all the priests rose and respectfully welcomed him. Bali also rose and greeted the newcomer in great happiness, offering him a seat, then washing his feet as is proper in receiving a respectable guest. Remembering how Shiva had sprinkled the water from Vishnu's feet on his head, he sprinkled Vamana's foot wash water on his own head.

(18.29) He felt a spontaneous attraction for the small boy arise in his heart. Without first consulting Shukra, he said, "O brahmin, I offer you my hearty welcome and respectful obeisance. I think you must be the personified austerity of great brahmin sages. Please let me know what I can do for you."

Vamana raised his right hand in blessing, smiling at Bali, who felt surges of joy.

(18.30) "My Lord," Bali said, "because of your arrival here, I feel as if my entire dynasty has been sanctified, and the sacrifice we are performing is already complete because of your presence.

(18.31) "Indeed, I think my fire sacrifice must be successful, for immediately on pouring the water that washed your feet on my head, I felt released of all the sinful reactions of my life. What to speak of me, I think the touch of your small feet can sanctify the entire world."

Vamana smiled charmingly and held out his begging bowl.

(18.32) Bali laughed. "If you have come here to ask for charity, you may have whatever you want. Take a cow, gold, a furnished house, food and drink, the daughter of a brahmin for your wife, prosperous villages, horses, elephants, chariots, and whatever else you desire."

Shukra stared suspiciously at the dwarf brahmin. Who was this person stealing his disciple's affection from him? He was certainly not Sanat Kumara, for Shukra knew him well. He had never seen this person before.

His influence and charisma were unprecedented. Could it be Indra in disguise? Or maybe Vishnu himself? Shukra sat in silent thought.

19
Vamana Begs Charity

(19.1-2) Vamana appeared delighted by Bali's greeting. He replied, "O great king, it is hardly surprising you are so pious. After all, your advisors are Bhrigu's brahmin descendants. I am sure that guided by your peaceful and venerable grandfather, Prahlada, your future life will be most exalted. All you have told me is true and completely in keeping with religious principles and your family's reputation."

A young assistant brahmin attending Bali whispered to his friend, "Why is he glorifying Prahlada? Despite being old, he is still attached to his family, especially King Bali."

His friend scowled and whispered back, "Don't be so foolish! Have you never noticed how Prahlada is never disturbed? This is only possible for someone advanced in transcendental science who has awoken his devotion to the Lord. Why! Prahlada is fit to be anyone's guru!"

His friend blushed and focused on what the young brahmin boy was saying.

(19.3-4) Vamana smiled up at Bali. "In your family, there have never been mean-minded people who refuse to give charity, nor have there been any misers who, after promising a gift, renege on their promise.[97] The kings in your dynasty have always given alms to brahmins living in holy places and agreed to fight when challenged by another warrior. King Prahlada shines in your family like a full moon, enhancing your dynasty's fame.

(19.5-6) "My dear king, your good qualities are hardly surprising considering that you come in the line of the heroic Hiranyaksha. Armed with only a club, your renowned ancestor wandered the globe alone; without assistance, he conquered all directions. No hero could rival him. Lord Vishnu finally killed him while assuming the form of a boar to rescue the earth, but not without difficulty. It is well known that whenever Vishnu remembers that encounter, he considers himself lucky to have emerged victorious."

(19.7-9) "Everyone has heard how your great grandfather, Hiranyakashipu, fearlessly stormed Vishnu's residence seeking revenge for his brother's death. Even though Vishnu is the best of all mystics, fully cognisant of past, present and future, he tried to hide from him. He was so sure that Hiranyakashipu would pursue him to his death that he decided to hide in his heart. Vishnu knew that was the only place Hiranyakashipu would not think to look for him, as he never introspected."

(19.10-13) Vamana chuckled. "I have heard that Hiranyakashipu ran with such speed that Vishnu panicked. In great anxiety, he assumed an inconceivably subtle body and entered Hiranyakashipu's nostrils along with his breath. When Vishnu suddenly disappeared, Hiranyakashipu screamed in a fury. Undeterred, he searched the entire universe in all directions, but unable to find Vishnu anywhere, he finally concluded he must be dead. Most people would stop feeling angry if they thought they had defeated their enemy, but that was not the case with your great-grandfather. He never gave up his anger toward Vishnu."

(19.14-15) Vamana became absorbed in thought. When he again spoke, his voice was full of tenderness. "Your father, King Virochana, so much loved brahmins that he gave his life to his enemies, the gods when they approached him in that guise. (Appendix C) You also have correctly observed the principles taught and followed by great householder brahmins, by your forefathers and by heroes famous for their piety."

(19.16) Vamana looked Bali straight in the eye. "O king of the Daityas, from your majesty, who comes from such a noble family and who can give charity munificently, I ask only three paces of land to measure my steps."

Bali's eyes widened. Three paces of land, as measured by Vamana's small steps?! He opened his mouth to reply, but before he could say anything, Vamana said, "This will be enough space for me to build a small hermitage for myself. Since I eat only what I am given in charity, I do not need land for agriculture."[98]

"I own the very cosmos!" exclaimed Bali. "Surely you can ask something more befitting of me?"

(19.17) Vamana said, "It is true that you control the universe. I also know you are extremely generous and capable of giving me as much land as I desire. However, I do not want to take anything from you which is not strictly necessary for my maintenance. You see, my dear king, if a learned brahmin takes charity only according to his needs, he does not become entangled in sinful activities."

(19.18) Bali was utterly charmed by Vamana's sweet speech and innocent request. "O brahmin, your words are as good as those of learned and elderly persons. Nonetheless, you are a boy, and your intelligence is not yet fully developed. Thus, you are not sufficiently shrewd regarding your self-interest."

Vamana blushed and looked down.

(19.19) Worried he might have hurt the boy's feelings, Bali quickly added, "Try to understand: I own all the universal planets and would willingly give you one. Since you have come to ask me for charity and pleased me with your sweet words, do you think it is in your best interest to ask me for only three paces of land? Of course not! That is what I meant when I said you are not being intelligent."

(19.20) Bali squatted in front of Vamana. "My dear boy, one who approaches me for alms should never have to ask anything more from anyone else again. Therefore, if you wish, you may ask from me as much land as will suffice to maintain you according to your needs for the rest of your life."

(19.21-22) Vamana gazed steadily at Bali. "My dear king, even the entirety of whatever may be within the three worlds cannot satisfy a person whose senses are uncontrolled. If I were not satisfied with three paces of land, which is all I need, then surely I would not be satisfied with one of the planetary systems. A greedy person always wants more."

Sensing his disciple and indirectly himself were being criticised, Shukra decided it was time to intervene, but Vamana continued before he could do so.

(19.23) "I have heard that past kings such as Prithu[99] and Gaya,[100] who ruled the entire universe, were still dissatisfied with their dominions."

Shukra settled down, feeling assured the boy's disparaging comments were not aimed at him or his disciple.

(19.24) Vamana continued to address Bali, who still squatted next to him. "My dear king, I have also heard that one should be satisfied with whatever he achieves by his previous destiny, for discontent can never bring happiness. A person not self-controlled[101] will not be happy even possessing the three worlds."

Bali listened intently. The boy's words made him reflect. He owned the three planetary systems, and yet he was not happy. He had always thought that once he defeated Indra and took over the universe, he would be content, but it was not the case. Why? Why did he still feel driven to achieve more?

(19.25) As if in answer to Bali's thoughts, Vamana said, "One in material consciousness thinks that fulfilling desires for more and more wealth is the path to happiness. They are simply entangling themselves further in the cycle of repeated birth and death. On the other hand, when we learn to be satisfied with what comes to us of its own accord, we attain liberation from material existence."

(19.26) Vamana glanced at the brahmins flanking Bali. "Satisfaction is crucial for a brahmin. If he is content with whatever he gets by providential arrangement, he becomes increasingly enlightened with spiritual power. On the other hand, the spiritual strength of a dissatisfied brahmin decreases, as fire is extinguished by water."

Shukra and the other brahmins looked irked by the boy's comment, but Vamana seemed not to notice.

(19.27) Turning back to Bali, Vamana concluded, "Therefore, O king, from you, the best of those who give charity, I ask only three paces of land. By such a gift, I shall be pleased, for the way of happiness is to be fully satisfied to receive only what is needed."

(19.28) Bali stood up and smiled. The boy had spoken wisely. "I agree. Take whatever you wish."

"Kindly confirm your promise in the customary way," said Vamana innocently.

Shukra stiffened. If the boy only wanted three paces of land according to his measurements, why was he asking for confirmation of Bali's promise?

Bali just laughed and reached for his waterpot.

(19.29) Shukra frowned. Of course! This was Vishnu. Only he could have spoken in such a way. He had to stop Bali from falling into his trap.

(19.30-31) He caught hold of Bali's right hand, in which he now held his waterpot. "Stop!"

Pulling Bali to the side, he whispered, "Listen to me, king. This *brahmachari* is certainly Vishnu, the imperishable Supreme Person. He has accepted Kashyapa and Aditi as his parents to fulfil the interests of the gods. You have put yourself in great danger by promising to give him land. If you follow this promise, you and the Asuras will suffer greatly."

Bali looked disbelievingly at the young brahmin child, who looked back with a look of unconcerned candour. "O Gurudeva, surely you are mistaken. He is just an innocent young ascetic."

(19.32) Shukra huffed. "Do not be fooled by his deception. This is Vishnu. He has falsely disguised himself as a dwarf *brahmachari* to steal everything from you. He will rob you of all your land, wealth, beauty, power, fame, and education and give it all to your sworn enemy, Indra."

"I have only promised him three steps of land," said Bali.

Shukra's nostrils dilated, and he seemed about to explode. If Bali went through with this promise, not only would he lose everything, but so would Shukra and his family. After all, their material prosperity depended on Bali's charity.

(19.33) "Ha!" he scoffed. "You have promised to give him three steps of land in charity, but when you give it, he will occupy the three worlds. You are a fool! You do not know what a great mistake you have made. After giving everything to Vishnu, you will have no means of livelihood. How then shall you live?"

Bali looked at the young boy, who sat peacefully awaiting his response. Surely Shukra was mistaken. Bali tried again to reason with his spiritual master. "I have never broken my promise. How can I do so now?"

(19.34) Shukra went red with fury. "Believe me, you will not be able to keep your promise!"

Bali looked baffled. "I own the entire universe. How will I not be able to give him three steps of land?"

"Because, you fool, with his first step, he will occupy the three planetary systems; with his second step, he will occupy the remainder of outer space."

Bali looked at the small dwarf. "How? He's so small."

"Listen to me, Bali. He will expand his body to occupy everything in the universe. There will be no place left for him to take his third step!"

"But I have already promised," said Bali in confusion.

(19.35) "I am telling you there is no way you will be able to fulfil your word. If you do not heed my warning, you will end up in hell for breaking a promise you confirmed."

"Should I not at least try to fulfil it to avoid sin?"

(19.36) "Hear me!" snapped Shukra impatiently. "Those who are learned in the Vedas do not recommend giving charity which endangers one's livelihood. Lacking the means to maintain yourself, you will be unable to perform any religious function like giving in charity, performing sacrifices, meditation,[102] or any worldly duties. If you knew scripture, you would know the importance of dividing your accumulated wealth into five parts. One part should be used for performing your religious duties, another for increasing your reputation, still another for increasing your opulence, the fourth for sense gratification, and the fifth for maintaining family members.[103] Following this advice will make you happy in this life and the next."

Bali remained unconvinced. "Since I have already promised, how can I now refuse? Surely that would be sinful!"

(19.38) Shukra spoke in a low voice. "Just tell him you are unable to go through with the promise."

"I control the universe! How can I tell him I cannot give him three steps of land?"

"Listen to what the Vedas say!" rejoined Shukra. "A promise does not count if not preceded by the word Om. Just tell him you do not have the land to give."

"I would be lying, and that is definitely a sin."[104]

(19.39-40) Shukra snorted. What was wrong with Bali? Could he not see his imminent destruction? Shukra took a deep breath to calm himself. "My dear Bali, you must be able to maintain yourself to gain the benefit of your human form of life. You cannot practise religion, study scripture, or even attain liberation if you do not maintain your body. Therefore, if to protect your body, you sometimes need to tell a little lie, so be it. Consider this example; if you uproot a tree, it will wither and die. Similarly, if you neglect the body, it will wither and die. Sometimes, to protect the body, you need to tell an untruth.[105] This is such an occasion. With a healthy body, one can become powerful, famous and fortunate. It is said that the fruits and flowers of the body are truth, although its root is untruth. Just as a tree with its root uncovered dries up and dies, by speaking lies, one uproots the body, and it dries up and dies. Therefore, one should not speak untruth unless it is to protect the body. Then one must."[106]

(19.41) Shukra looked sternly into Bali's eyes. "You are not yet obliged to give anything. Only when you precede your promise with the word Om must you give what you pledged. Do not foolishly promise to give everything. You will become penniless, and that is not a good position for you. That is why I instruct you not to utter the word Om. If you do not heed my advice, you will lose everything and be unable to attain either self-realisation or material happiness."

(19.42) Shukra pulled Bali closer and whispered into his ear. "The best way out is to say that you cannot afford to give him what he wants. That is always a good way to avoid giving charity. It attracts the compassion of others and can even inspire them to give charity to you."

Bali's agonised features betrayed his perplexity. Previously, Shukra had always insisted he give him in charity whatever he promised. He said, "Should I always lie like this?"

"Of course not. If you always plead you have nothing, you will be condemned," he said. "You will be no better than a dead body even though alive, and you will deserve immediate death." He cited Vedic evidence to support his argument.[107]

Bali looked from Shukra to Vamana, who seemed wholly undisturbed and detached. It did not make sense that he could not lie to Shukra, but he could to this young *brahmachari*.

(19.43) Noting Bali's indecision, Shukra tried again to dissuade him. "Listen to me, Bali. According to scripture, there are occasions when lying is permissible. You can lie without incurring a sin to court a woman, as a joke, to praise the groom in a marriage ceremony, to earn your livelihood, to protect yourself when you are in danger, to protect cows and brahmins, or to protect someone from an enemy. On such occasions, falsity is never condemned. Believe me, king, this situation is dangerous, and there is no sin in you lying."

20
Bali Surrenders the Universe

(20.1) Bali remained silent for some time. He owed much to Shukra, who had brought him back from the dead and by whose grace he had gained universal supremacy. Bali had served Shukra unswervingly for many years because he knew that he would achieve all good fortune by satisfying the spiritual master. How could he now disobey him?

He looked across at Vamana, who had not shown the slightest disturbance as Shukra spoke. Would it be right to break his promise to such a self-controlled brahmin? To lie or fail to honour a promise given to a brahmin was always condemned. If the boy was Vishnu, he had more reason to keep his promise. Bali could see no justification to deny Vamana's request.

The Daitya king inwardly wrangled with his dilemma. He was faced with choosing between the offence of disobeying his spiritual master or lying to a brahmin. He needed to think clearly. Bali glanced at Shukra, who scowled back. Was his guru giving proper guidance? He had always engaged him in performing sacrifices in which Vishnu was honoured. By so doing, Bali had become victorious over all his enemies and had achieved fabulous wealth. Yet now,

Shukra wanted him to disregard Vishnu. It seemed his guru's intention throughout was material gain. If this was Shukra's thinking, then there was no sin in rejecting him. One should never be led by a person only interested in his own gain. A genuine spiritual master must train his disciples to satisfy the Supreme Lord. Shukra had clearly lost his discrimination, so there would be no fault in disobeying him.

(20.2) Placing his palms together, Bali addressed Shukra, "Dear brahmin, you have told me that one should follow a religious principle only when it does not hinder one's self-interest. I accept this principle."

Shukra let out a sigh of relief. Bali had seen sense.

(20.3) Bali took a deep breath. Over the years, he had developed much affection and respect for his spiritual master. It was not easy for him to now defy him. "My dear sir, I do not think breaking my word to this brahmin out of greed for money is in my best interest. I am the grandson of the famed King Prahlada. How can I disgrace myself and him by behaving like an ordinary cheater, especially toward a brahmin?"

Shukra's face turned red. "What? Do you think following my order would disgrace you and turn you into an ordinary cheater?" he exclaimed, jumping to his feet.

(20.4) Bali mustered his courage. "My lord, there is nothing more sinful than untruthfulness. The earth goddess once said, 'I can bear any heavy burden except a liar'."

"You fool! I already explained this to you. You will not be able to fulfil your promise and descend into hell."

(20.5) Bali's expression was solemn. "I do not fear hell, poverty, an ocean of distress, falling from my position or even death itself as much as I fear cheating a brahmin."

Shukra shook his head in despair. "You will lose everything!"

(20.6) Bali had made up his mind. He would give Vamana anything he asked for, even if he was Vishnu.[108] Nevertheless, he wanted to placate his spiritual master if possible. "My lord, you know better than I do that all one's wealth is lost at death. Therefore, is it not better that I try to satisfy this brahmin with the riches that I am destined to lose?"

Shukra glared at Bali. Fire seemed to emanate from his eyes and nostrils, so great was his wrath. "You are the only fool in human history who thinks it noble to give away everything in charity!"

(20.7) Bali remained calm. "Dadhichi, Shibi and many other great personalities were willing to sacrifice even their lives to benefit others. So why not give up this insignificant land? What is the objection?"

"You are a Daitya, Bali," said Shukra in tightly constrained tones. "Act like one. Do you think your great ancestors Hiranyaksha and Hiranyakashipu would approve of your decision?"

(20.8) "O best of the brahmins, certainly the great Daitya kings who were never reluctant to fight enjoyed this world, but in due course of time, everything they had was taken away, except their reputation by which they continue to exist. Therefore, one should try to achieve a good reputation only."

Shukra pointed an accusatory finger at his disciple. "You will be known as a loser, a fool! That will be your reputation Bali!"

(20.9) Bali spoke humbly. "How is that possible, my dear brahmin? Many heroes have gained fame by laying down their lives in battle. Rare is that hero who gets the chance to give his accumulated wealth faithfully to saintly persons. Such persons attain even greater fame."

"You will become poverty-stricken!"

(20.10) "If I became poor due to gambling, intoxication, or other such reasons, then I would certainly be blameworthy.[109] Becoming poor due to giving all my possessions in charity to a saint of your calibre will enhance my reputation. Therefore, I am determined to give this little *brahmachari* whatever charity he asks of me."

Shukra shouted in frustration. "This is no ordinary *brahmachari*. This is Vishnu! He has come on behalf of your enemies to trick you. He will rob you of everything!"

Bali looked at Vamana, who silently observed the exchange between him and his guru.

(20.11-12) Then he turned to Shukra and spoke in a conciliatory tone. "Great sage, saintly persons like you know full well that all rituals and sacrifices must be performed for Vishnu's pleasure. If this boy is indeed Vishnu, is that not even more reason to give him anything he asks for, regardless of whether he intends to bless or punish me? Indeed, my reputation would be greatly enhanced if Vishnu, out of fear, disguised himself as a brahmin to beg from me. Under the circumstances, I will not retaliate, even if he irreligiously arrests or even kills me. It makes no difference whether he is my enemy or not."

(20.13) Trying one last time to pacify Shukra, Bali said, "If this is the mighty Vishnu, he would never give up his widespread reputation through such deception. He would challenge me to a fair fight and either kill me or be killed by me."

Tears pricked Bali's eyes as he looked affectionately at Vamana. How could he ever kill him? Vishnu could not be slain by anyone, even if they were foolish enough to try.

(20.14-15) Shukra stood with clenched fists glowering at Bali. Unable to contain himself, he vehemently spat out a curse. "Thinking yourself magnanimous and fixed in truthfulness, you dare disobey my order! You have no knowledge, yet you pose as a learned person and impudently defy me. Because of this serious transgression, you shall very soon lose everything."

(20.16) With these words, Shukra stormed back to his seat. Bali was visibly shaken. He owed so much to Shukra. It was deeply saddening that he had been unable to appease him. He again glanced at Vamana, who smiled. The Daitya king did not regret his decision. According to custom, he washed Vamana's hands with water from his waterpot before affirming his promise.

(20.17) Meanwhile, Bali's wife, Vindhyavali, who was seated behind a curtain, shed tears of joy. It was so wonderful to see her husband's firm devotion to Vishnu. She stepped out and told the maidservants, who were coming forward with a golden pot of water, to give her the container.

The maidservants gaped in surprise. One said to another, "This is remarkable. Our lady is so chaste that she has never been seen in public. How is it that now before everyone's vision, she wishes to assist with this *brahmachari's* foot bathing?"[110]

(20.18) Bali took the golden water pitcher from his wife and washed Vamana's feet in great jubilation. When the foot bathing was finished, he sprinkled the foot water on his head. If this was truly Vishnu, then the water could deliver the universe.

(20.19) Witnessing Bali's unpretentious surrender to Vishnu, the gods, Vidyadharas, Siddhas, Charanas and Gandharvas loudly praised him. They all appeared in the skies above and showered him with flower petals while jubilantly chanting, "All glories to the ever-truthful King Bali!"

(20.20) The Gandharvas, Kimpurushas, and Kinnaras came down, beating thousands of kettledrums and blowing trumpets. They danced and sang jubilantly. "King Bali is truly an exalted soul. What a difficult task he has performed. Even though he knew Lord Vishnu was on the side of his enemies, he gave him the three worlds in charity."

(20.21) The young dwarf *brahmachari* began to expand his size unlimitedly. Bali looked up in astonishment. He saw that the entire universe, including the planets, outer space, seas, gods, sages and all species of life, sat in Vamana's body.

Bali murmured, "Since I have already decided to give you anything you ask for, you are free to increase your size as much as you wish."[111]

(20.22) As Bali, his priests, Shukra, and everyone else present watched, Vamana manifested his universal body, replete with his six famous excellences.[112] They saw that along with the different species, it also comprised the gross material elements, the senses, sense objects, mind, intelligence, false ego, and the three modes of nature.

Marvelling at this spectacular sight, Bali exclaimed, "Now I see that everything in the universe exists in your body. I cannot give you anything since you already possess everything. Nevertheless, just as the Ganges accepts her own water from her devotee, kindly accept my offer."

(20.23-24) Vamana endowed Bali, seated on Indra's throne, with a mystic vision by which he could see everything. Bali first saw the feet of Vishnu's universal form. On the soles, he saw the lower planetary systems such as Rasatala;[113] on the dorsum of Vishnu's feet, he saw the surface of the earth; on his calves were the mountains; on his knees, an array of birds, and on his thighs were the winds. On Vishnu's garments, Bali saw twilight; on his private parts, the Prajapatis; on his buttocks, he saw himself and his chief associates;[114] on the Lord's navel was the sky; on his waist were the seven oceans; and on his bosom rested all the constellations.

(20.25-29) Bali gaped in wonder. This was undoubtedly the all-powerful Lord Murari, who slew the invincible Mura Asura. (Appendix D) On his heart, he saw religion; on his chest were pleasing words and truthfulness; in his mind was the moon; on his bosom sat the goddess of fortune holding a lotus flower; on his neck, he saw the Vedas and all the syllables[115]; on his arms, the gods headed by Indra; in both his ears were the directions; on his head rested the upper planetary systems; on his hair, the clouds; through his nostrils blew the raging wind; in his eyes, he saw the sun, and in his mouth was fire. When he spoke, his words were Vedic mantras. On his tongue, Bali saw Varuna, the god of water. As Bali glanced further up, he saw religious rules and prohibitions sitting on Vamana's eyebrows When he opened his eyes, it became day, and when he blinked, it became night. On his forehead rested anger, and greed lingered on his lips. Bali sensed that the universal form's touch was the source of lusty desires, and that his semen was that of water. On his back was irreligion, and Bali saw the fire of sacrifice when he moved or took a step. Death personified stood in the Lord's shadow and the illusory energy was in his smile. His bodily hairs were medicinal herbs, and the rivers were his veins. Stones came from his nails, and Brahma, the gods and the sages from his intelligence. Bali could see all living entities moving and stationary throughout Vishnu's fantastic form.

(20.30) Bali's Asura followers saw Vamana holding the Sudarshana disc and a mighty bow. Feeling the intolerable heat generated by the disc and hearing the tumultuous sound produced by the twanging of his bow, they shook with fear.

(20.31) As everyone stood unmoving in astonishment, Krishna's conch, Panchajanya, his club, Kaumodaki, his sword, Vidyadhara, his quiver, Akshaya-sayaka, and his shield decorated with many moons, all appeared in their personified forms to praise Vamana.

(20.32-34) They were accompanied by Narayana's associates from Vaikuntha, like Sunanda and Nanda, and the predominating gods of the various planets. Together, they glorified Vishnu, who wore a brilliant helmet, bracelets, and glittering fish-shaped earrings. He then assumed another wondrous and gigantic form. His bosom was decorated by a lock of hair, which Bali knew was called Shrivatsa, and the Kaustubha gem; he was dressed in yellow g   arments   held in place with a belt and decorated with a flower garland surrounded by bees. In this form, he took his first step, which covered the entire surface of the earth, while his body and arms filled the sky and all directions. With his second step, he covered all the higher planets, including Satyaloka. There was nowhere left for him to place his third step.

21
Bali Arrested

(21.1) When Vamana's foot reached Brahma's planet Satyaloka, the effulgence emanating from his nails outshone its brilliance. With bowed heads, Brahma and the celestial sages headed by Marichi, along with yogis like Sanandana, all came forward to worship Vamana. Those effulgent sages seemed like candles before the sun.

(21.2-4) Brahma began to recite choice prayers, and many other great personalities hurried forward to worship Vamana's upraised foot with oblations of water. Among those who came were the personified Vedas and their corollaries,[116] and the saintly residents of Brahmaloka. The water washing Vamana's foot flowed down from the sky as the sacred Ganges River to sanctify the universe.

(21.5) His mission accomplished, Vamana reduced his all-pervading form and again manifested himself as a dwarf *brahmachari*. Brahma then led the leaders of all the planets in performing his formal worship ceremony.

(21.6-7) While the gods played musical instruments, danced, and sang prayers glorifying Krishna's pastimes, Brahma performed formal worship. He offered Vamana fragrant flowers, water to drink, and to wash his hands and feet,[117] followed by offerings of incense, lamps, fused rice, unbroken grains, fruits, roots and sprouts.

(21.8) When news reached Jambavan, the king of the bears, that Vishnu had appeared as Vamana, he hurried there as swift as the mind,[118] loudly resounding his bugle. "Let there be a festival celebrating Lord Vamana's victory!" he declared.

(21.9) Bali's Asura followers, however, were outraged. Their glorious master had been determined to perform the sacrifice, yet Vamana cheated him of everything on the pretence of begging three paces of land.

(21.10) They angrily berated Vamana. One growled, "This Vamana is certainly not a brahmin, but the greatest cheater, Vishnu."

Another indignantly added, "The wily Vishnu has disguised himself to work for the gods!"

(21.11) The Daityas huddled together to discuss the situation. One said, "It is not right for one performing a religious sacrifice to punish wrongdoers at that time. Taking advantage of this, our eternal enemy Vishnu has assumed the dress of a *brahmachari* beggar to steal away all our king's possessions."

(21.12) Another added, "He knows our lord, Bali, is truthful and will never break his promise, especially while he is engaged in sacrifice. Not only will he never lie, but he is always merciful toward brahmins. Aware of this, that cunning Vishnu is robbing him!"

(21.13) Their fury and indignation mounted until one of them finally said, "Since our master is bound by virtue not to punish Vishnu for his treachery, it falls on us. We must kill him. This is our only religious option, and we will thereby serve our master."

All the Daitya generals raised their weapons and yelled, "Kill Vamana! Kill Vamana!"

(21.14) The battle cry rippled through the ranks of disgruntled Daitya soldiers. They gripped their lances and tridents and advanced on Vamana. Seeing this, Bali called out, "Stop! Stop!" His pleas fell on deaf ears.

(21.15-17) The four-armed Vaikuntha associates of Vishnu unsheathed their weapons and stood between the advancing Asura horde and their Lord.

Nanda, Sunanda, Jaya, Vijaya, Prabala, Bala, Kumuda, Kumudaksha, Vishvaksena, Garuda, Jayanta, Shrutadeva, Pushpadanta and Satvata, each of whom was as powerful as ten thousand elephants, began slaughtering the fierce Daitya army.

(21.18-19) Bali watched in dismay as his soldiers were slain in the thousands by the invincible associates of Vishnu. Remembering Shukra's curse, he rushed forward to intervene. "Viprachitti! Bana! Nemi! Please hear my words! Cease fighting! The present time is not in our favour."

Restrained by their king, the Asuras lowered their weapons, but their chests still heaved with anger.

(21.20) Bali sympathetically counselled them. "O Daityas, by no means can anyone overcome the Supreme Person since he has the power to bring happiness and distress to all living entities. My dear friends, previously, we could defeat the gods because Vishnu favoured us in his form as time. This is no longer the case."

One general objected, "Maybe Shukra can find a way to overcome the time factor. After all, he previously brought you back from the dead!"

(21.22) Bali shook his head. "My friend, no one can surpass the supreme time factor by material power, the counsel of ministers, intelligence, diplomacy, fortresses, mystic mantras, drugs, herbs or by any other means."

The Asura generals scowled. "Why not? If he can defeat death, he can defeat time!"

Others nodded and grunted their agreement.

Bali sighed. There was no point trying to explain this philosophically. He would have to keep his points simple.[119]

(21.23-24) "Listen to me. We were previously able to defeat Vishnu's followers because Providence empowered us."

He pointed to the gods, who were laughing and rattling their weapons. "See how those same followers are now beating us and roaring in jubilation like lions. We cannot defeat them until Providence again favours us. So best we bide our time."

One general said, "We can't just stand by and watch this injustice toward you!"

Bali placed a hand on his shoulder. "I will be fine. Wait in the lower planets until you hear from me."

(21.25) The soldiers looked up at their master, whom they had vowed to obey. Then they glanced at Vishnu's followers, who brandished their weapons menacingly. Without another word, they turned and entered the lower regions of the universe.

(21.26) Garuda stepped forward and began to bind the unresisting Bali with ropes. As Vishnu's eternal carrier, Garuda understood his master's mind well. He knew that Vishnu was not satisfied to take Bali's possessions but wished to accept Bali's very self, thus glorifying his devotion and tolerance.[120]

(21.27) The Asuras, watching from the lower planets, and the gods all protested. "Why is Vishnu arresting this virtuous king? He does not deserve such treatment!"

Bali's wife, Vindhyavali, cried in anguish, "Please do not harm him!"

(21.28) The sages praised Bali. "This Bali is a most liberal and celebrated personality," they said.

Vamana walked up to the tightly bound Bali, who stood with downcast eyes, his clothes dishevelled, and his bodily lustre wholly gone.

"So," said Vamana. "Do you intend to keep your promise?"

"Yes," replied Bali. "I am a man of my word."

(21.29) "O king of the Asuras," said Vamana. "You promised me whatever I can cover in three steps. However, I have already occupied the entire universe with only two steps. Tell me where I can place my third."

Bali hung his head as Vamana went on.

(21.30-31) "This entire universe belongs to you, but with one step, I occupied all the planets up to the earth, and I occupied the entire sky and all directions with my body. You saw that I occupied the entire upper planetary system with my second step."

He spread his hands as if to say, "So where shall I put my third step?"

Bali looked confused. "What should I do? I have given you all I possess!"[121]

(21.32) Vamana's expression was grave. "The ordained punishment for not keeping one's promise is that one must go to hell. Since you cannot give charity according to your promise, you should go live on the hellish planets. You may ask your learned guru Shukra if what I say is true or not.[122] If he confirms my words, you should immediately go to hell and live there."

Bali turned to Shukracarya, who nodded to confirm Vamana's words. No one spoke; only Vindhyavali's loud sobs broke the shocked silence.

(21.33) Looking out at the assembly of mystified celestials and brahmins, Vamana said, "Far from being elevated to the heavenly planets or fulfilling one's desire, one who does not properly give a supplicant what he has promised falls to a hellish condition of life."

(21.34) He again addressed Bali, "Falsely proud of your possessions, you promised to give me land, but you could not keep your word. Therefore, because your promise was false, you must live for some time in hell."

22
Bali Surrenders

(22.1) Bali kept his head bowed. How could he break his promise? His reputation for being truthful would be destroyed. That would be worse than going to hell. Better to surrender to Lord Vishnu and somehow fulfil his promise. Vishnu was merciful. Many Daityas had attained a destination greater than most mystic yogis simply by their enmity toward him. Bali thought of his grandfather Prahlada and his great determination in devotional service. By his complete surrender, he had become glorious. Bali had to follow his example.[123] That was the only choice left.

(22.2) Lifting his head, he smiled and said, "My Lord, most venerable one, if you think my promise has become false, I shall rectify matters to make it truthful, for I cannot tolerate breaking my word. Please, therefore, place your third lotus footstep on my head."

Vamana also smiled. "So you think like this I will have you untied, and you will not go to hell?"[124]

(22.3) Bali shook his head. "No, Lord. I do not care that you have taken everything from me, nor do I mind that you have bound me, and I am not concerned about going to hell. However, I fear losing my good reputation and being branded a liar."

Vamana said, "Has not being bound up like a common criminal already diminished your reputation?"[125]

(22.4) Bali said, "Although a father, mother, brother or friend may sometimes punish one for one's good, their punishment is never as severe as what you have meted out to me. However, since you are my revered Lord, I regard my punishment at your hands as supremely auspicious."

Vamana frowned. "Why do you think like this? I am famous for helping the gods, not you Asuras."[126]

(22.5) Still bound tightly hand and foot and barely able to keep his balance, Bali humbly replied, "I consider you a better friend to the Asuras than to the gods."

"Oh, how is that?"

Bali replied meekly. "You act for our best welfare by posing as our enemy. You thereby deprive us of our false prestige, which causes our bondage. I consider it your great favour to us Asuras that you humble us since humility is the first prerequisite for transcendental knowledge.[127]

Vamana laughed. "You consider me your well-wisher, even though I killed your ancestors Hiranyakashipu and Hiranyaksha?"

(22.6-7) "They were constantly inimical toward you, but when killed by you, they achieved the same perfection as great mystic yogis. Your acts bring about only good for all living beings. Therefore, even though you have severely punished me, I am neither upset nor ashamed."

Vamana replied, "How do you have such faith in me, despite my ill-treatment of you, Bali?"

(22.8) Bali said, "I remember the counsel Grandfather Prahlada always gave me. He is famous as your great devotee because although continuously tortured by his father Hiranyakashipu, he never lost faith in you, considering you the only true shelter for all living beings."

Vamana nodded his head by way of expressing his appreciation of Prahlada's devotion. "Why do you think Prahlada chose to surrender to me over obeying his father?"

"Because he was most intelligent."

"How was that?"

(22.9) "The relationship between father and son is based on the body, but we are not these material bodies, and after we die, we will cease to have any further connection with either our bodies or relatives connected to these bodies."

"That may be true after death, but surely family members are more important than others during one's life."

Bali grunted. "Humph! What use are family members? They drain a man of all his wealth."

"Oh, but surely they are a source of pleasure," said Vamana. "Consider your wife, for example; she must give you so much happiness."

Bali smiled, "Yes, but she has also increased my material entanglement. A married man is responsible for providing his children a suitable home and other social amenities. Consequently, he feels obligated to maintain relations with other people in the community. All this wastes one's valuable human energy, which is meant to cultivate pure devotion for you.

(22.10-11) "King Prahlada, being very knowledgeable, understood this and was wary of materialistic association. He surrendered to you despite his father's opposition because he knew this was the most auspicious course, and now he is highly revered by all while his father is dead, slain by you. It is my good fortune that you have forcibly overpowered me and taken away my opulence. Ephemeral material wealth deludes people, making them forget their precarious situation in this material world, that we can die in an unforeseen accident at any moment. By good fortune, you have saved me from this illusion."

(22.12-13) While Bali was speaking, Prahlada appeared there. He illuminated the assembly like a full moon rising at night. Dressed in elegant yellow silken garments, he was tall with long graceful arms, a dark complexion, and beautiful eyes resembling lotus petals.

(22.14) Bali wanted to make his prostrate obeisance, but being tightly bound, he could only bow his head. He blushed with deep shame. His saintly grandfather always tried to give him good advice, but he had neglected it out of pride. Now, look at his position. His esteemed grandfather would surely think his arrest was due to some grievous offence.[128]

(22.15) Prahlada peered around the assembly, trying to ascertain who was responsible for his grandson's arrest. When he saw Vamana surrounded by his Vaikuntha associates, he immediately recognised him as the Supreme Personality. Prahlada felt his skin horripilate, and tears of jubilation flowed from his eyes. He fell to the ground before Vamana.

"Welcome, my dear devotee, Prahlada. Have you come to plead on behalf of your grandson?" Vamana asked.

(22.16) Kneeling on the ground before Vamana, with his palms placed together, Prahlada said, "My Lord, you previously gave Bali his opulence, and now you are taking it back. I think this is your great mercy. Because his exalted position as king of heaven made him forget life's real value, you have rendered him a great favour by confiscating his wealth."

(22.17) Turning to Bali, Prahlada said, "My dear grandson, material affluence is so bewildering that it makes even a learned, self-controlled man forget to pursue self-realisation. Narayana, the Lord of the universe, desiring only your good, has taken everything away."

Bali nodded, "Thank you, Grandfather; by your grace, I can understand this truth."

Embracing Bali, Prahlada once again bowed to Vamana and stood respectfully to one side.

(22.18-19) Brahma, who was sympathetic to Bali, had hoped his grandfather would secure his release. Prahlada had not asked for this, so he felt impelled to intervene. He was about to speak when Vindhyavali, Bali's wife, stepped forward, afraid and aggrieved about her husband's condition. After making her obeisance to Vamana, she knelt before him and, with folded hands and tears streaming down her face, spoke prayerfully.

(22.20) "My Lord, you have created the entire universe to enjoy your pastimes, but foolish, unintelligent men like my husband, desiring to exploit your property, claim proprietorship. Certainly, he has acted like a shameless unbeliever. He is so foolish; he believed that the universe belonged to him and that he could give you charity. Everything, including our bodies, belongs to you alone."

Vindhyavali broke down crying, and Vamana smiled kindly at her.

(22.21) Brahma stepped forward and respectfully addressed Vamana. "O well-wisher and master of all living entities, worshipful Deity of the gods, all-pervading Personality of Godhead, this man has been sufficiently punished, for you have taken his all. Kindly release him. He does not deserve to be punished more."

Vamana smiled at Brahma, "Welcome, Lord Brahma. How is it that you, the chief of the gods, plead on behalf of this reprobate chief of the Asuras? Even his grandfather has not asked for his release. Why do you think he does not deserve further punishment?"

(22.22) Brahma said, "My Lord, King Bali has already offered you everything. Without hesitation, he gave his land, the planets and whatever else he earned by his pious activities, including his body. One can achieve the highest position within the spiritual world even by sincerely offering you water, grass, or flower buds. Without deceit, Bali offered everything in the three worlds. How does he deserve to suffer arrest?"

(22.24) Vamana addressed Brahma in stern tones. "You think he does not deserve further punishment? My dear Brahma, because of material opulence, foolish people like Bali become dull-witted and mad. They lose respect for even the gods, thus defying my authority. It is my special kindness when I take everything away from such arrogant persons."[129]

Feeling admonished, Brahma respectfully bowed his head and stepped back with folded hands.

Turning to Garuda, Vamana ordered, "Bring me the prisoner."

Garuda dragged the bound and unresisting Bali before the Lord, who addressed him in severe tones. "Bali, do you know for how long you have been rotating in the cycle of birth and death?"

Bali stood with his head lowered, feeling too ashamed to speak.

(22.25-27) "Again and again, you have passed through all the different species of life. Finally, by good fortune, you have obtained a rare human birth. Those I especially favour do not become proud despite possessing all material opulence. Normally, aristocratic birth, personal beauty, good education and wealth cause a person to become falsely proud. If my devotee remains humble despite possessing such opulence, I generally do not take it away since he will not use it to degrade himself."[130]

Bali bowed his head. How shameful was his position. Yet the Lord had undoubtedly shown him kindness by saving him from the madness of his pride. It must surely be because of his love for his saintly grandfather that Vamana personally rescued him from the illusion of material enjoyment.

Everyone waited in silence for Vamana to continue. What would he decide? Would Bali be banished to the hellish planets?

"Garuda!" Vamana called out in a commanding voice. "Release the prisoner."

The whole assembly exploded in shouts of joy and relief. Now free, Bali bowed before Vamana and waited for his command.

(22.28) With a smiling countenance and a voice softened with affection, Vamana addressed the assembly, "This King Bali has become the best among the Asuras. Although I have taken everything from him, he remains unperturbed and fixed in his promise. Even though bereft of his riches, fallen from his position, defeated and arrested by his enemies, rebuked and deserted by his relatives and friends, suffering the pain of being bound, and censured and cursed by his spiritual master, he has remained fixed in truth. Earlier, when I said he had acted irreligiously by failing to keep his promise[131], I spoke deceptively; he has not abandoned religion, for he is true to his word."

Everyone jubilantly chanted, "All glories to Lord Vamana! All glories to King Bali!"

(22.31-32) After a few moments, Vamana raised his hand, and the assembly again became quiet. He addressed Brahma and the assembled celestials, "Because of his great tolerance, I have awarded Bali a place not obtainable even by you gods. Later, during the reign of Savarni Manu, he will become Indra, the king of heaven. In the meantime, he will reside on the planet Sutala which Vishvakarma made according to my specifications. It is hundreds of times better than heaven. Protected by me, it is free from mental and bodily miseries, fatigue, defeat and all other disturbances. He may live there peacefully. Not even the gods will be able to trouble him there, for I will personally become his doorkeeper and always guard him."[132]

The Gandharvas beat drums, Apsaras danced, and the gods looked one to the other, amazed by Bali's good fortune. Bali sat in stunned silence. How quickly his situation had changed. His grandfather had been right. One is never a loser by surrendering to the Supreme Lord.

(22.33-34) Vamana then turned and addressed Bali.[133] "My dear King Bali, with your family and friends, you may now go to Sutala, which is desired even by the gods. There you will enjoy great fortune. While you rule over this planet, no one will be able to conquer you, not even the gods. As far as the Asuras are concerned, if they transgress your rule, my disc will kill them."

Bali fell to his knees before Vamana and said, "My Lord, now that you have destroyed my illusion born from bad association, please do not again put me in a situation where I may become proud. I desire to remain your devotee."

(22.35-36) Vamana held up a reassuring hand. "O great hero, do not fear anything. I shall remain with you and protect you in all respects, along with your associates. You will see me always, and by my grace, you will never again be placed into illusion, despite your association with the Asuras."

23
The Heavens Regained

(23.1) Tears streamed from Bali's eyes. How great was his good fortune. The Lord had accepted him as his pure devotee, a position only attained by highly exalted souls. He addressed Vamana in a voice faltering with devotional ecstasy.

(23. 2) "My dear Lord, when you first appeared in the sacrificial arena, I immediately wanted to bow down to you, but I dared not out of fear of displeasing Shukra and my Asura associates; but now I see that just because I wanted to offer you my obeisance, I have attained such a wonderful result, just like that attained by your pure devotees."

Vamana said, "Are you referring to the fact I gave you Sutala as your residence?"

"Oh no, my Lord! Your real mercy is that you placed your lotus foot on my head.[133] Such grace has never been attained even by the gods or leaders of different planets."

(23.3) Bali made his prostrated obeisance first to Vamana and then to Brahma and Shiva. Then he joyfully entered Sutala.

(23.4) Vamana then approached his mother, Aditi. "O mother of the gods, your son Indra may now resume his rulership of the heavens."

The celestials cheered and glorified Vamana. "Just see how expertly the Lord manages universal affairs!" they exclaimed.

(23.5) Prahlada had listened quietly while Vamana spoke to Bali. Now that everything was settled, he stepped forward to offer his prayers.

(23.6) Prahlada's heart overflowed with feelings of ecstasy, his bodily hair stood erect, and his voice quavered. Wiping the tears from his eyes, he said, "O supreme shelter of everyone, even great personalities like Brahma and Shiva worship your lotus feet. I am astonished that out of everyone here, it is us Asuras you have promised to protect. I do not think you have ever shown such kindness to anyone, not even to Lakshmi, the goddess of fortune, what to speak of the celestials or common people."

Vamana looked curiously at Prahlada. "Why do you say I have never shown such mercy to anyone? Have I not just returned the heavens to the celestials?"

(23.7) Prahlada said, "Oh, I know you have bestowed vast wealth and many powers to the celestials like Brahma and others. However, they have rendered much devotional service to you to attain this mercy. On the other hand, we Asuras are rogues and debauchees, always envious of others. I am astonished you would show us such great mercy. It is completely causeless."

Vamana smiled, appreciating Prahlada's words. Then assuming a perplexed look, he asked, "So do you think I failed to deal with everyone equally? Did I show favouritism to the Asuras?"

(23.8) Prahlada chuckled. "My Lord, since you are all powerful, your pastimes defy logic. You are simultaneously equal to all while also showing favouritism."[134]

"Oh? How am I equal to all?"

"You are equal in three ways: everyone's body in the material world is created by your material energy; you know everything about everyone, and you are the source of their consciousness and life energy."

Vamana nodded approvingly and then asked, "So how do you think I display favouritism?"

"Among all the living entities you have created, you show affection for your devotees and not for others."

"Surely this is a fault in me!" exclaimed Vamana.

"Not at all!" replied Prahlada. "This is a great quality. Just as a desire tree fulfils the desires of all who take shelter of it, and not of those who do not, similarly you fulfil the desires of devotees who take shelter of you, and not of others."

(23.9) Vamana smiled, satisfied with Prahlada's reply. He said, "My dear son Prahlada, all good fortune unto you. For the time being, you also go to Sutala and enjoy happiness with your grandson, other relatives and friends."

Prahlada's face darkened with worry. "My Lord, out of fear of bad association, I have stayed aloof from the company of the Asuras for many years now."

(23.10) Vamana reached out and took Prahlada's hand. "Dear Prahlada, your presence will be very good for Bali and his followers. You have nothing to fear, for you shall always see me in my Vishnu form with conch, disc, club and lotus in my hands. Because of the transcendental bliss of perceiving me, you will never fall prey to materialistic activities."

(23.11-12) Prahlada bowed his head in submission. "As you wish, my Lord."

He walked around Vamana three times, offered his prostrated obeisance again, and left for Sutala.

(23.13) Vamana now looked around the assembly of celestials and brahmins. Seeing Shukra sitting nearby with the other sacrificial priests, he said, "Ah! Here are the knowers of the Vedas!"

At Vamana's signal, Shukra came forward without hesitation. He had nothing to fear. Vishnu was known as Hari, or he who removes one's offences. If he had committed any offence, Vamana would surely find a way of relieving him of it because of his connection with Bali.[135]

(23.14) Vamana said, "O best of the brahmins, Acharya Shukra, kindly tell me for what fault did you curse your disciple King Bali?"

Shukra took a deep breath. "My Lord, since the king is not present here to defend himself, I feel hesitant to accuse him of any fault."

Vamana replied, "There is no need for Bali's presence, for his faults and discrepancies can be nullified if judged before the brahmins."

(23.15) Shukra spoke in a voice full of contrition. "My Lord, you both establish the sacrificial rules and enjoy its results. If one fully satisfies you, there is no question of him making any mistakes in performing sacrifice. The fault was mine for having wrongly chastised and cursed him. Please forgive me."

Vamana smiled, "You may complete Bali's sacrifice now. If there were any discrepancies in its performance, please rectify them. Let it be done perfectly."

Shukra looked up timidly into Vamana's face. Tears of relief and gratitude welled up in his eyes. The Lord was allowing him to redeem himself.

(23.16-17) "My Lord," Shukra said in a faltering voice, "even if there were discrepancies in pronouncing the mantras and observing the regulative principles regarding time, place, person and paraphernalia, just by chanting your holy name, everything was rectified. Still, I shall obey your order, which is most auspicious and the prime duty of all."

(23.18) Shukra bowed to Vamana and returned to his seat by the sacrificial fire. With the assistance of the other priests, he began to compensate for the omissions in Bali's sacrifices.

(23.19) When the ritual was complete, Vamana beckoned Indra to come forward.

"My dear brother, Indra. As requested by our mother, Goddess Aditi, I have retrieved your kingdom. I now return it to you."

(23.20-21) Brahma, Shiva, the assembled gods, sages, Pitris, Manus and universal progenitors all collectively called out, "All glories to Lord Vamana!"

Brahma said, "To bring pleasure to Kashyapa Muni and his wife Aditi and to do good to all the inhabitants of the universe, you have acted expertly for everyone's protection."

(23.22-23) With the unanimous support of everyone present, Brahma continued, "It is true that Indra is the king of the universe, but we all request that you remain with us to protect the Vedas, religious principles, our fame, opulence, auspiciousness, vows, and the process of elevation to the higher planets and liberation. Lord, we all accept you as the supreme master of everything."

Vamana smiled in acquiescence, and the assembly erupted into a spontaneous display of joy.

(23.24) Amid much singing, dancing, and playing of musical instruments, and with the approval of

Brahma, Indra invited Vamana to ascend his celestial aircraft.

(23.25) Indra was especially delighted that Vamana had agreed to return to Amaravati with him. Everything had turned out better than before. He was reinstated in his post, and Lord Vamana now protected him. As he ascended the aeroplane after the Lord, he felt supremely opulent, fearless and fully satisfied.

(23.26-27) Brahma, Shiva, the celestial sages, Pitris, Siddhas and all the other celestials present loudly sang Vamana's glories as Indra's celestial plane soared toward heaven. When Vamana had departed, they also returned to their respective planets, all the while speaking about Vamana and glorifying Aditi's good fortune in having attained him as her son.

***

"All glories to Lord Vamana!" exclaimed Parikit, his mind stunned with wonder. As a king, he had seen how hard it was to resolve long-standing disputes and enmities. One party or the other would inevitably feel dissatisfied. Yet the Lord acted so wonderfully that everyone's faith, love and satisfaction increased. He thought over how Vamana had spoken to Bali, Prahlada, Indra, and the errant Shukra, to whom he had displayed such kindness. Whether stern or liberal, the Lord acted perfectly and thereby liberated everyone, including those who had only heard about the event.

(23.28) Shukadeva sat with his eyes closed for a few moments, relishing the memory of Vamana's pastime. Then opening his eyes, he addressed Parikit, "My dear king, I have now described everything about the wonderful activities of the Supreme Lord, Vamana. Those who hear about this are freed from all sinful reactions."

***

"How glorious!" exclaimed Shaunaka. "Just by hearing about this astonishing pastime, the beleaguered people of this age can benefit supremely. What need is there for any other welfare work?"

One sage looked doubtful. "Did Shukadeva mean it literally when he said, 'Hearing this narration frees you from all sins'?"

Shaunaka looked up at Suta, waiting for his response.

(23.29-30) "My dear sages," said Suta, "hear from me this verse which Shukadeva quoted and which was originally composed by Vasishtha Muni. 'No one who takes birth in the material world can measure the glories of Lord Vishnu.' Let me assure you, dear sages, if one hears about the extraordinary activities of the Supreme Lord in any of his various incarnations, he is certainly elevated to the higher planetary systems or even the supreme Vaikuntha planets."

The sages called out, "Wonderful! Wonderful!"

(23.31) Suta continued, "Shukadeva further declared that if Lord Vamana's pastime is recited at any ceremony, whether it be for material gain, to please Krishna, or simply a social custom such as a birthday celebration, that ceremony will become most auspicious, and all present will be greatly benefited."

Shaunaka said, "It was certainly providential grace that sent you to us, dear Suta. Before your arrival, we were most anxious about the future. You have given us great hope that we can bring relief to any soul in Kali Yuga who desires their good. If it pleases you, pray tell us more about the conversation between those two great souls, Parikit and Shukadeva."

24
Matsya, the Divine Fish.

Shukadeva said, "I have described the fourteen Manus in the current day of Brahma and the histories of Krishna's incarnations during each of their reigns. Is there anything else you would like to know?"

Parikit thought for a few moments. Repeatedly Shukadeva had stressed the importance of hearing about Krishna's divine activities. Parikit loved these pastimes as they gave him great solace. He cast his mind back over all he had heard and decided he would like to know more about Matsya, the fish incarnation, whom Shukadeva had already briefly mentioned.[136]

(24.1-3) "My dear master, I have learned from you that although the Lord is always transcendentally situated, he nevertheless regularly descends to the material world in various forms. I have heard that his first incarnation was as Matsya, the fish. O most powerful sage, kindly tell me more about that pastime. I am confused why he would accept the form of a fish. Conditioned souls are forced to accept such a low body due to past sins, but I don't understand why the Supreme Lord accepts such an abominable form. Fish suffer greatly and always face peril, so why would Krishna accept such a form? He must have done so to favour some devotee, and I am eager to know more about that personality.[137] Since hearing about Krishna's pastimes is auspicious for everyone, kindly explain all this to me."

(24.4-5) Shukadeva showed his appreciation for the question. "I am delighted that you have inquired about Matsya. First, however, let me establish the universal truths about the Lord's incarnation. He incarnates to accomplish one or more of these goals: to protect cows, brahmins, the gods, his devotees, the Vedic literature, religious principles and those required for attaining the goal of life.

(24.6) "Secondly, the Lord's forms are never abominable, but always transcendentally situated.[138] Consider this example; the air passes through many places but never changes. Even though it may carry a strong odour, it still does not change its nature. Similarly, even when the Lord accepts the form of a fish, his transcendental nature is not compromised."

(24.7-9) (24.57) The sage explained that Krishna had twice incarnated as a fish. "At the end of Brahma's last day, at the time of annihilation, a demon stole the Vedic knowledge. Thus, at the beginning of Brahma's new day, when Svayambhuva Manu commenced his reign, the Lord appeared as Matsya and rescued the Vedas. Later, Matsya again appeared during the reign of the sixth Manu, Chakshusha."

"My dear master, pray tell me about that second appearance."

(24.10) Shukadeva replied that there lived at that time a king named Satyavrata, who was Vishnu's great devotee.

"Listen now as I tell you his history."

King Satyavrata knelt on the bank of the River Kritamala, offering oblations to Krishna. He was always happiest when engaged in such worship. Disinclined toward worldly enjoyment, he had only assumed kingship of the world to please his father, who had wished to retire. Seeing Satyavrata unmarried and without issue, his ministers had repeatedly beseeched him to accept a wife. Therefore, the king decided to engage in the austerity of subsisting only by drinking water whilst meditating on Vishnu to gain his favour.

(24.12-14) He continued his worship for some months. One evening as he scooped up the river water in his cupped hands, he saw he had caught a small fish. As he was about to throw it back into the river, to his surprise, the fish spoke in an appealing voice. "My dear king, protector of the poor, why are you throwing me in the river where other aquatics can kill me? I am very much afraid of them."

(24.15) Startled, the king looked down at the unusual fish and said, "O small fish, you are my subject, and I must offer you protection. You have no reason to be afraid."

(24.16) Keeping the fish safely in his hands, he waded back to shore, where his charioteer stood, ready to return him to the palace. Ordered by Satyavrata, the charioteer quickly filled his water jug with clear river water. With the fish safely placed within, the king returned to his palace along with the tiny creature.

Early the following day, before the sun had risen, King Satyavrata worshipped the brahmins and dealt with the matters of state his ministers brought before him. An hour after sunrise, he prepared to return to the River Kritamala to continue his meditations. Before leaving, he decided to check on the fish. He said to an attendant, "Bring me the fish I brought back last night."

(24.17-18) The servant ran off and returned with the jar containing the fish. The king saw it had grown so much during the night that it could not move. In an anguished voice, it said, "My dear king, please help me. This water pot is far too small for me. I am in great discomfort. Please find some better vessel where I can reside peacefully."

(24.19) Snatching the jar from the servant, Satyavrata hurried to a nearby large well and threw the fish in. Peering into the well, the king called, "Dear fish, be peaceful and happy here. I will check on your comfort again when I return from my meditations this evening."

(24.20) Turning to leave, he only took a few steps when he heard the fish plaintively calling out, "Please help me. This well is not big enough for me. Please give me a more extensive pool of water, for I have taken shelter of you."

Perplexed, the king turned back and again peered into the well. The fish was now so large that he could barely move in the well. Satyavrata shook his head in amazement. He had to move the fish immediately, but how? It could not be lifted with the well bucket. He would need to call the court brahmins to extract the fish using mantras. The king despatched his servants to summon the brahmins swiftly. He stayed by the well, consoling the distressed fish.

(24.21-22) When the priests arrived, Satyavrata said, "Good sirs, please transport this fish to the palace lake with all haste."

Surrounding the well, the chief and most experienced brahmins began chanting mantras in unison. Suddenly before the king's eyes, the fish disappeared from the well. Accompanied by his entourage, he hurried to the lakeside in his palace gardens. Satyavrata's eyes widened with alarm when he saw from a distance a gigantic aquatic splashing its tail in distress, barely able to move in the lake. Seeing the king hurrying toward him, the fish called out, "Dear king, save me. I am far too large for this pond. Please find a larger lake where I may live comfortably."

Turning to the brahmins and his court ministers, the king anxiously said, "This fish has taken shelter of me. I cannot disgrace my dynasty by allowing it to die. Which of you can advise me of a suitable body of water where this creature may peacefully live under my protection?"

(24.23-24) As the ministers looked at each other in bewilderment, the brahmins quickly conferred. Then the chief brahmin addressed King Satyavrata, "Dear king, there is a large lake in a valley not far from here, where sages go to perform austerities. It is extensive, and there are no dangerous aquatics dwelling there. This is the most suitable place for us to transport this creature."

"Do it immediately!" the king ordered.

Ascending his chariot, he hurried to ensure the fish was safe. By the time he arrived at the lakeside, along with the brahmins and his court ministers, the fish had already grown too large for even that vast reservoir. His head painfully pressed against the bank, he called out pitifully when he saw the king's chariot racing toward him.

"O king, thinking you were a righteous monarch, I sought your shelter. Why have you put me into such a miserable condition?"

Sweat pouring from his brow, the confounded king alighted from his chariot and surveyed the situation. This lake was like a small sea, but the fish's body was so massive that it could hardly move. Addressing the fish, which continued to reproach him, he said, "Dear fish, please be patient. I shall immediately have you transferred to the vast ocean."

Ordered by Satyavrata, the brahmins again began to chant their mystic mantras. Still, on hearing them do so, the fish cried, "O hero, do not throw me into the great ocean where there are very powerful and dangerous sharks that will eat me."

The brahmins desisted and waited for the king's order. Satyavrata fell to his knees by the lakeside, his head in his hands, his mind bewildered. How could he, the great and powerful Satyavrata, not be able to give suitable protection to a fish?

(24.25-26) Finally composing himself, the king addressed the fish in a humbled voice, "Who are you, sir? We are confused. You have expanded for hundreds of miles in one day, covering the river and ocean water. Before this, I had never seen or heard of such an aquatic animal."

The fish did not reply but thrashed about in the lake, repeating, "I have sought your shelter. You must save me."

Satyavrata wrung his hands in anguish. How had this fish so confounded him? He prayed to Vishnu. Surely this phenomenal creature was the Lord himself. Satyavrata's heart became gladdened as this realisation dawned. Yes, this was clearly Vishnu removing his pride in being a great ruler and protector of others. He began offering heartfelt prayers to the divine aquatic.

(24.27-28) "My Lord, you are undoubtedly the inexhaustible Supreme Personality of Godhead, Narayana. You have assumed a fish form to show us mercy. You are the master of creation, maintenance, and annihilation, the supreme enjoyer, Lord Vishnu. You are the leader and destination of surrendered devotees like us. Therefore, I offer you my respectful obeisance."

The fish replied in a grave and sonorous voice, "Why do you think I am Vishnu? Could I not be a god?"

Satyavrata's conviction increased, and tears of joy began to trickle down his cheeks. "My Lord," he said, "I have never worshipped the gods. Since they falsely identify with their material bodies, worship of them is fruitless in all respects. I have always worshipped the Supreme Lord, Vishnu, because he is the greatest friend and dear most Supersoul of everyone. Such worship is never useless. Therefore, I am certain you are my venerable Lord appearing as a fish."

(24.29-30) The enormous fish gave a great booming laugh, indicating his approval of Satyavrata's words. Still kneeling by the riverbank, Satyavrata humbly placed his palms together and addressed Matsya. "All your incarnations certainly appear for the welfare of all beings. Therefore, my Lord, I wish to know why you have assumed this aquatic form."

(24.31) Again Matsya's melodic laughter resounded across the lakeshore, bringing joy to the hearts of all. "My dear devotee, I have come to do you good and enjoy my pastimes in the waters of the inundation."

Satyavrata looked perplexed, "Inundation?"

(24.32-33) "My dear hero, do not be afraid. Seven days from today, the three planetary systems will all be annihilated. You need have no fear, for I will send you a large boat."

(24.34-35) Satyavrata listened attentively to Matsya's instructions to collect every herb and seed and load them on that great boat. He should also gather a male and female from every species.

"I shall instruct the seven great sages to accompany you. With their companionship, you will be free of all moroseness."

(24.36-37) Matsya warned Satyavrata that powerful winds would toss about the boat, but he should not fear. "I shall assist you, and the great serpent Vasuki will also come to you. Tie one end of his body around my horn and the other to the boat. Pulling that ship with you and all the sages in it, O king, I shall swim in the water of devastation until Brahma's slumber ends."

Satyavrata's heart filled with sorrow and compassion. How could he save himself and let all the world's citizens perish in the flood?

The king said, "I would rather die with everyone else than live in the knowledge that I did not protect my citizens from this impending destruction."

(24.38) Matsya said, "It is only due to illusion that you feel such grief. While I guide you through the seas, I will favour you with transcendental knowledge, freeing you of all lamentation and fear."

(24.39-40) Matsya then disappeared. The king immediately ordered his ministers to gather the seeds of all the herbs and vegetation, along with males and females of all species and bring them to him. He spread *kusha* grass in that same spot, sat on it, and meditated on Matsya.

(24.41-42) As Matsya had predicted, after one week had passed, huge dark clouds gathered in the sky and poured water incessantly, swelling the ocean more and more. Soon everywhere was flooded as the seas swept over the land. Satyavrata continued to sit amid the deluge, determinedly meditating on Matsya. On his order, sages descended from the higher regions to join him. As the flood waters rose, a great boat appeared before them. Satyavrata and the sages quickly loaded all the animals and seeds onto it and climbed aboard.

(24.43) The rains relentlessly beat down, and fierce winds tossed the boat from side to side. The sages gathered around Satyavrata, and shouting over the howling wind, they asked him to again meditate upon the Supreme Lord, Keshava.

"He will save us from this impending danger and arrange for our well-being."

(24.44-45) Satyavrata sat below deck, meditating upon Krishna. The boat rocked back and forth, and the sea swept over the deck, threatening to engulf them, but Satyavrata still did not break his meditation. After a few days and nights had passed, during which Satyavrata continuously meditated, a gigantic golden fish appeared in the storm-tossed ocean. The fantastic creature's length could not be estimated. The sages thought it stretched for millions of miles. They also saw that it had a single great horn on its head. The serpent king Vasuki also appeared in the swirling ocean along with Matsya.

In a trance, Satyavrata heard Matsya say, "My dear devotee, open your eyes and quickly secure the boat to my horn."

Returning to external consciousness, Satyavrata rushed up on deck and saw Matsya playing in the waters. He also saw Vasuki lifting his tail out of the water and over the ship. Along with the sages, the king wrapped it around a great bollard in the boat's prow. Vasuki then coiled himself around the divine fish's horn. As Matsya began to heave on the ship, it steadied amid the wind and rain. Satyavrata collapsed on the deck, his heart pounding. They were safe at last. He remembered his ministers and citizens as he recovered from the previous week's ordeal. They had all depended on his protection, but now they were all dead, drowned in the floods. His heart ached, and he wept aloud, his copious tears mixing with the pounding rain. How would he ever find relief from this terrible heartache?

Recalling Matsya's reassurance, he composed himself and went to the ship's forecastle. He stood with folded palms and in a voice hoarse with grief, called prayerfully to Matsya.

(24.46-54) "My dear Lord, since time immemorial, I have forgotten my real self and falsely identified with my material body. Thus, I have suffered unbearable miseries. O Lord Matsya, I accept you as the supreme spiritual master. Please cut the knot of illusory desires for material happiness from my heart. No one else, neither gods nor the sages, can offer mercy that equals yours. Therefore, I surrender unto you. (Appendix E) Please enable me to realise my true eternal spiritual identity. O Lord, most dear friend, supreme controller, by your instructions, please enable me to understand life's true purpose."

(24.55) On hearing his devotee's sorrowful prayer, Matsya compassionately began to instruct him about the difference between the body and the soul. He cited histories from the Puranas, his voice carrying powerfully over the howling winds and rain, carefully explaining that the soul's real interest lies in surrendering to him with love and faith.

(24.56) As Satyavrata, surrounded by the sages, listened to Matsya's instructions regarding self-realisation, all his sorrow gradually dissipated.

***

Parikit listened in silence. Tears of gratitude pricked his eyes, which he fixed on Shukadeva with affection and reverence. Just as Matsya delivered King Satyavrata from ignorance and dissipated his grief, the sage, as the Lord's perfect representative, was delivering him.

Shukadeva said, "My dear king, I have now explained why Krishna incarnated as a fish. Do you have any other questions?"

Parikit gathered his thoughts. He had doubts about the Matsya episode.

The king said, "O master, Satyavrata lived during the reign of Chakshusha Manu, the sixth in this day of Brahma. Normally annihilation occurs after the fourteenth Manu, at the end of Brahma's day. How is it that an inundation occurred after the sixth Manu?"

"An excellent observation and question, dear Parikit."

Shukadeva explained that this devastation occurred not during Brahma's night but during his day. "By Krishna's supreme will, Brahma felt sleepy and took a short rest during his day. It was the Lord's inscrutable desire to favour Satyavrata by delivering transcendental knowledge to him."

Parikit shook his head slowly in amazement. To elevate his devotee, Krishna can even contravene the cosmic order. "Dear master, pray tell me, what happened to Satyavrata after the inundation subsided?"

(24.11) (24.58) "Completely illuminated with Vedic knowledge by the mercy of Lord Matsya, he later took birth as the son of Vivasvan, the sun god. He now lives as the Manu of this current age, Vaivasvata."

(24.59-61) Shukadeva concluded, "The story of Matsya is a great transcendental narration. Anyone who hears it is delivered from the consequences of sinful life. He will have all his ambitions fulfilled and return to the spiritual world. I offer my humble respects to Lord Vishnu, who pretended to be a fish, explained the essence of Vedic literature, and returned that knowledge to Brahma after it had been snatched by a Asura named Hayagriva."

***

The sun was setting over Naimisharanya as Suta ended his narration for the day. The sages gradually rose from their places and went to the Gomati River for their evening bath and prayers. The air was filled with the buzz of their conversation.

"Such fascinating stories," said one. "The Lord's pastimes are truly astonishing."

"Indeed," said his companion. "And just by hearing them, we can be liberated."

"Yes," said a third sage, overhearing them. "How wondrous. No need for rigorous austerity, yoga or great Vedic scholarship. Just hear about Krishna."

Loudly praising Krishna, the sages entered the river and began their prayers, looking forward to the next day when Suta would resume his narration.

END

Appendix A: The fourteen Manus and the gods, sages, and Vishnu Avatars in their reigns

(Collated from chapters 1, 5, and 13)

Chapter / Verse	Name and number of Manu and his father	Manu's children	Indra and gods and seven sages during his reign (where named)
1.1-6 (See also Vidura's Pilgrimage 12.56-57)	1st: Svayambhuva. Father: Brahma	Priyavrata, Uttanapada, Akuti, Devahuti, Prasuti	Indra: Yagya
1.19-22	2nd: Svarochisha Father: Agni	Dymat, Sushena, Rochishmat and others	Indra: Rochana (Yagya's son) Gods: Tushita and others Sages: Urja, Stambha, and others
1.23-26	3rd: Uttama	Pavana, Srinjaya,	Indra: Satyajit

	Father: Priyavrata	Yagyahotra and others	Gods: The Satyas, Vedashrutas, and Bhadras. Sages: Vasishta's sons headed by Pramada
1.27-30	4th: Tamas Father: Priyavrata	Prithu, Khyati, Nara, Ketu and 6 other sons	Indra: Trishikha Gods: Satyakas, Haris, Viras. Vaidhritis Sages: Jyotirdhama and others
5.2-5	5th: Raivata Father: Priyavrata	Arjuna, Bali, Vindhya and other sons	Indra: Vibhu Gods: Bhutarayas Sages: Hiranyaroma, Vedashira and Urdhvabahu

5.7-9	6th: Chakshusha Father Chakshu	Puru, Purusha, Sudyumna and other sons	Indra: Mantradruma Gods: The Apyas Sages: Havishman and Viraka
13.1-6	7th: Shraddhadeva [1] Father: Vivasvan	Ikshvaku, Nabhaga, Dhrishta, Sharyati, Narishyanta, Nabhaga, Dishta, Tarusha, Prishadhra, Vasuman	Indra: Purandara Gods: The Adityas, Vasus, Rudras, Vishvadevas, Maruts, Ashvini-kumaras, and Ribhus Sages: Kashyapa, Atri, Vasishtha, Vishvamitra, Gautama, Jamadagni, Bharadvaja
13.11-17	8th: Savarni Father: Vishvakarma	Nirmoka, Virajaska, others	Indra: Bali Gods: The Sutapas, Virajas, and Amritaprabhas

			Sages: Galava, Diptiman, Parashurama, Ashvatthama, Kripacharya, Rishyashringa, Vyasadeva
13.18-20	9th Daksha-savarni Father: Varuna	Bhutaketu, Diptaketu, others	Indra: Adbhuta Gods: The Paras and Marichigarbhas Sages: Adbhuta, Dyutiman, others
13.21-23	10th Brahma-savarni Father: Upashloka	Bhurishena, others	Indra: Shambhu Gods: The Suvasanas, Viruddhas and Others. Sages: Havishman, Sukrita, Satya, Jaya, Murti, others

13.24-25	11th: Dharma-savarni Father not named	Satya-dharma & 9 other sons	Indra: Vaidhrita Gods: The Vihangamas, Kamagamas, Nirvanaruchis, others Sages: Aruna and others
13.27-29	12th: Rudra-savarni Father not named	Devavan, Upadeva, Deva-shreshtha, others	Indra: Ritadhama Gods: Haritas and others Sages: Tapomurti, Tapasvi, Agnidhraka, others
13.30-32	13th: Deva-savarni	Chitrasena, Vicitra, others	Indra: Divaspati Gods: Sukarmas, Sutramas and Others Sages: Nirmoka, Tattvadarsha,

			others
13.33-35	14th: Indra-savarni Father not named	Uru, Gambhira, Budha, others	Indra: Shuci Gods: The Pavitras, Cakshushas + others Sages: Agni, Bahu, Shuci, Shuddha, Magadha, + others

1. Another name for Shraddhadeva Manu is Vaivasvata Manu. See SB canto 9, chapter 1 Introduction: "Śrāddhadeva, or Vaivasvata Manu, the father of Mahārāja Ikṣvāku…". He is the current Manu. See SB 1.3.12 purport: "…the present period is of Vaivasvata Manu…"
2. He was Dhruva's great grandson. (see Sarartha Darshini, note to 8.5.7)
3. Savarni's mother was Chaya, Vishvakarma's second wife. See SB 8.13.8 & 10

Appendix B: Progeny of the sun god Vivasvan with his three wives: Samjna, Chaya, Vadava

Vivasvan's wife	Her father	Her sons	Her daughters
Samjna	Vishva karma[1]	Yama, Yami, Shraddhadeva[2]	
Chaya	Vishva karma	Savarni,[3] Shanaishcara (aka Saturn)	Tapati (married King Samvarana)[4]
Vadava		The twin Ashvini brothers	

1. One of Daksha's 61 daughters was Vasu who married Yamaraja. One of their sons was Vastu who married Angirasi. Vishvakarma, the gods' architect, was one of their sons. (See Divine Protection, appendices A & B & C)
2. Shraddhadeva is another name for Vaivasvata Manu. (See SB 9.2.1 verse)
3. This Savarni becomes the eighth Manu. (See SB 8.13.11)
4. King Samvarana and his wife Tapati are the parents of King Kuru, after whom the Kuru dynasty is named. (See SB 9.22.4-5)

Appendix C: Chapter 19 text 14: Virochana's death.

There are two different statements about the death of Virochana in the Puranas.

(1) In the battle with Tārakāsura, Virochana was killed by Devendra. (Mahābhārata Śānti Parva, Chapter 99; Brahmanda Purana 1. 20. 35; Matsya Purana 10: 11; Padma Purana Sristi Kanda 16).

(2) The sun god was pleased with Virochana and gave him a crown that protected him from death. Because of this boon Virochana became arrogant. So Vishnu took the form of a beautiful woman and enticed Virochana toward him and, taking away the crown, killed him. (Ganesha Purana 2.29). According to Narada Purana (2.32), Vishnu took the form of a brahmin and approached Virochana. Changing Virochana's wife into a mad woman he had Virochana slain.

Appendix D: When will accepting a guru help or not help us?

When the guru has fully and correctly assimilated the science of Krishna:

"Whether one is a brāhmaṇa, a sannyāsī or a śūdra — regardless of what he is — he can become a spiritual master if he knows the science of Kṛṣṇa." CC Madhya 8.128 verse, (please see the purport to this verse also.)

This is only possible if we first cultivate our own sastric discrimination:

"Suppose you have to purchase some gold or jewelry, and if you do not know where to purchase, if you go to a grocer shop to purchase a jewel, oh, then you'll be cheated. If he says..., go to a grocer shop and ask, "Oh, can you give me diamond?" he will understand that "Here is a fool. So let him [me] give him something: This is diamond." "Oh. What is the price?" He can charge anything, and when you come home, your relatives say, "What you have brought?" "This is diamond. I went to the grocer shop." So that kind of finding spiritual master will not do. You have to become a little intelligent. Because without being intelligent nobody can make any spiritual progress." Srila Prabhupada Lecture on Bg 4.34, 12/08/1966; New York;

We can cultivate adequate sastric discrimination by thoroughly studying Bhagavad-Gita As It Is:

"Therefore without being intelligent you cannot make progress. Ignorance is the cause of all difficulties. So Bhagavad-gītā, if you have read Bhagavad-gītā, it is said there that Bhagavad-gītā is being preached to Arjuna, and Kṛṣṇa says that "I am teaching this Bhagavad-gītā again." Room Conversation with African Intelligentsia; 24/09/1971; Nairobi;

However, if we remain ignorant of Krishna's teachings in Bhagavad-Gita and choose a spiritual master based on external considerations such as the following, there is a chance we will be misled:

We may be misled if we select someone as guru simply because they have been appointed to that post:

"Self-deceived persons sometimes accept leaders or spiritual masters from a priestly order that has been officially appointed by the codes of material life. In this way, they are deceived by official priests." (Srila Prabhupada, Chaitanya-charitamrita, Madhya Lila 17.185 purport)

We may be misled if we select someone because of who their guru or family is, or because of social custom (e.g. it is customary to accept a sannyasi), or because of the rules set up by a priestly caste of an institution:

"It is imperative that a serious person accept a bona fide spiritual master in terms of the sastric injunctions. Sri Jiva Gosvami advises that one not accept a spiritual master in terms of hereditary or customary social and ecclesiastical conventions. One should simply try to find

a genuinely qualified spiritual master for actual advancement in spiritual understanding." (Srila Prabhupada, Caitanya-caritamrita, Adi 1.35 purport)

We may be misled if we accept a guru who uses his or her position to increase their material opulence or as a means of income for their personal or family's maintenance:

"One should not become a spiritual master for one's personal benefit, for some material gain or as an avenue of business or occupation for earning livelihood. Bona fide spiritual masters who look unto the Supreme Lord to cooperate with Him are actually qualitatively one with the Lord, and the forgetful ones are perverted reflections only." SB 1.13.48 purport

We may be misled if we take initiation prior to having controlled our own senses, or we accept someone as guru who has not fully controlled his or her senses:

"Therefore the so-called formal spiritual master and disciple are not facsimiles of Brahmā and Nārada or Nārada and Vyāsa. The relationship between Brahmā and Nārada is reality, while the so-called formality is the relation between the cheater and cheated. It is clearly mentioned herewith that Nārada is not only well-behaved, meek and obedient, but also self-controlled. One who is not self-controlled, specifically in sex life, can become neither a disciple nor a spiritual master. One must have disciplinary training in controlling speaking, anger, the tongue, the mind, the belly and the genitals. One who has controlled the particular senses mentioned above is called a gosvāmī.

Without becoming a gosvāmī one can become neither a disciple nor a spiritual master. The so-called spiritual master without sense control is certainly the cheater, and the disciple of such a so-called spiritual master is the cheated." SB 2.9.43 purport

Those who are truly masters in the science of bhakti advise the aspiring devotee not to neglect scriptural injunctions and proceed based on speculative ideas:

'The so-called path of *bhakti* practised by unauthorized persons without knowledge of *bhakti* may be easy, but when it is practised factually according to the rules and regulations, the speculative scholars and philosophers fall away from the path. Śrīla Rūpa Gosvāmī writes in his *Bhakti-rasāmṛta-sindhu* (1.2.101):

>śruti-smṛti-purāṇādi-
>pañcarātra-vidhiṁ vinā
>aikāntikī harer bhaktir
>utpātāyaiva kalpate

"Devotional service of the Lord that ignores the authorized Vedic literatures like the *Upaniṣads, Purāṇas* and *Nārada Pañcarātra* is simply an unnecessary disturbance in society."' Bg 7.3 purport

Appendix E: What does it mean to surrender to Krishna? (24.52)

"Sudāmā: Now, Śrīla Prabhupāda, Kṛṣṇa has sent you here to teach us this art of surrendering.
Prabhupāda: Yes.
Sudāmā: Now you have told us to first of all surrender. So as your students, we are trying to hear in that way. Now when we go and preach and we tell..., if we tell a man, "First of all, you surrender before you'll be able to understand," then what, what question is there of preaching?
Prabhupāda: They have already surrendered. They have already surrendered. When they have come to hear you, that is a symptom of surrender. Otherwise, why does he waste his time? There is little bit surrender. ***Full surrender and partial surrender. When one agrees to hear you, that is partial surrender.***" - Morning Walk, 10/12/1973; Los Angeles.

NOTES

1. "...the creation by Brahmā in each day of his life is called *kalpa*." SB 2.10.46 purport).
2. See Two Avatars 24.16)
3. See Krishna Fulfills All Desires 1.1-2)
4. "Among all the stories in which the Supreme Lord is glorified, this story bestows great purity, glory, auspiciousness and fortune." Sarartha Darshini 8.1.32
5. "He thought, 'This is my karma.'" Sarartha Darshini 8.2.31 commentary)
6. "Araṇi wood is a kind of fuel used to ignite fire by friction. At the time of performing sacrifices, one can ignite a fire from araṇi wood." Srimad Bhagavatam 4.16.11 purp.
7. The translation of Srila Prabhupada's Srimad Bhagavatam seems to suggest the Vedas are amongst the minor expansions. However, in his commentary Vishnvanatha Chakravarti Thakur writes, "The actions mentioned in the Vedas are created by the Lord. 'Veda' here means actions since the Vedas themselves are not minor expansions of the Lord. But rather the Vedas arise directly from his breathing." Sarartha Darshini 8.3.24
8. "Major expansions are Matsya, Kurma and others who are always the Supreme Lord. All of these are the Lord." Sarartha Darshini 8.3.24 commentary.
9. See Sarartha Darshini 8.3.25 commentary.

10. "I desire the freedom that is without destruction…" Sarartha Darshini 8.3.25 commentary.
11. "I do not have a way of attaining the Lord. The yogis, who are not like me (an animal), burn up all karma by bhakti-yoga." Sarartha Darshini 8.3.27 commentary.
12. "I surrender to the Lord of inconceivable power by whose energy this elephant does not know his own atma, which is overcome by the conception of false ego." Sarartha Darshini 8.3.29 verse.
13. "The devatas like Brahma, appointed by the Lord to protect the righteous, did not come ….They thought, 'Gajendra has not praised us at all, but rather belittled us, calling us minor expansions (verse 22). So let the Supreme lord whom he praised come for him. But he will not appear immediately. We know he is hard to attain by his nature. Therefore the elephant will die." Sarartha Darshini 8.3.30 commentary.
14. "Once Huhu, while playing in the water with some women, grabbed the foot of Devala and pulled it. Devala became angry and crused him. 'Become a crocodile!' But on being pacified by Huhu, he spoke. 'The Lord will free you when you attack Gajendra.'"
15. Srimad Bhagavatam 10.14.8 verse.
16. See Bhagavad Gita As It Is 18.66 verse.
17. "However, because in his mind a devotee may still maintain the remnants of his previous sinful mentality, the Lord

removes the last vestiges of the enjoying spirit by giving His devotee punishments that may sometimes resemble sinful reactions. The purpose of the entire creation of God is to rectify the living entity's tendency to enjoy without the Lord, and therefore the particular punishment given for a sinful activity is specifically designed to curtail the mentality that produced the activity. Although a devotee has surrendered to the Lord's devotional service, until he is completely perfect in Kṛṣṇa consciousness, he may maintain a slight inclination to enjoy the false happiness of this world. The Lord therefore creates a particular situation to eradicate this remaining enjoying spirit. This unhappiness suffered by a sincere devotee is not technically a karmic reaction; it is rather the Lord's special mercy for inducing His devotee to completely let go of the material world and return home, back to Godhead." SB 10.14.8 purport.

18. See Appendix A
19. "The *rishi* known as Śubhra, by his wife, Vikuṇṭhā, gave birth to the Supreme Personality of Godhead, Vaikuṇṭha." SB 8.5 introduction
20. See SB 8.5.5 purport & The Universal Order, chapter 20.34-39
21. See Appendix A.
22. "Well if no one is supposed to be killed, then why do we see killing?" He accepts rajas for creation and tamas for

destruction. This means that he accepts them, in the sense that he is non-different from his energies. By tamas, satta and rajas, he destroys, protects and disregards the living entities." Sarartha Darshini 8.5.22 commentary

23. "Though the Lord was present, he could not be seen except by his will." Sarartha Darshini 8.5.25 commentary
24. "He is transcendental to all material afflictions because He is full with all six opulences, namely wealth, power, fame, beauty, knowledge and renunciation, and thus He is the master of the senses." SB 1.3.36 purport.
25. "...the Lord who is manifested externally as time and internally as antaryami." Sarartha Darshini 8.5.31 commentary.
26. "Therefore, to gain this understanding, the demigods, headed by Lord Brahma, offered their respectful obeisances to the Lord." SB 8.5.31 purport.
27. See *Krishna Fulfills All Desires* Ch.24 verse 64.
28. See SB 8.5.32 purport.
29. See SB 8.5.33 purport.
30. "...which is the embodiment of the three Vedas," Sarartha Darshini 8.5.36 verse.
31. "...secondary life-airs..." Sarartha Darshin 8.5.38 verse.
32. "...from whose touch arose the desire for benefiting animals..." Sarartha Darshini 8.5.42 verse.
33. "'O Brahma! Please accept your desired boon.' Brahma answers: show your svarupa to us, who have surrendered to

you. 'Is this form without qualities or with qualities?' Show that form which we can perceive with our senses. It is a form with qualities. That form has a lotus face with a smile.'" Sarartha Darshini 8.5.45 commentary.

34. "Lord Brahma is eager to see the incarnation of the Lord, or the original source of all incarnations…" SB 8.5.46 purport.

35. "However, even if one does not perform actions (prescribed duties) but one worships the Lord, one receives all the results of all action. Without worship of the Lord, all actions are without result." Sarartha Darshini 8.5.49 commentary.

36. "When it first appeared in English in the 14th century, obeisance shared the same meaning as obedience. This makes sense given that obeisance can be traced back to the Anglo-French obeir, a verb meaning "to obey" that is also an ancestor of English's obey. The other senses of ***obeisance*** also date from the 14th century, but they have stood the test of time, whereas the "obedience" sense is now obsolete." https://www.merriam-webster.com/dictionary/obeisance.

37. "Whether you will fulfil our desire or not, we do not know. You are unlimited…. 'But because I am merciful, you can infer that I will fulfil the desires of Indra and other devotees.' By your merc you do not give material benefits ….which are obstacles to bhakti…. 'Why do you praise

me if you have such doubts?'" Sarartha Darshini 8.5.50 commentary.

38. "Lord Brahma, expressing his appreciation, said that because Lord Visnu had now taken charge of the activities of goodness, there was every hope that the demigods would be successful in fulfilling their desires....However, as Lord Brahma has previously described since the time of sattva-guna had now arrived, the demigods could naturally expect to fulfil their desires." SB 8.5.50 purport

39. "Because of the prayers offered by the demigods in the previous chapter, Lord Ksirodakasayi Visnu was pleased with the demigods, and thus he appeared before them." introduction to SB canto 8, chapter 6.

40. "He was worshipped by his weapons personified, such as the cakra." Sarartha Darshini 8.6.3-7 verse

41. You devatas are also famous as objects of worship.' True, but we are all included in your worship." Sarartha Darshini 8.6.9 commentary.

42. How can people see me?" Sarartha Darshini 8.6.12 commentary.

43. "You may say, 'You are not omniscient, but you are very intelligent and clever. So please tell the solution to this problem, so that even though you can do nothing, I can accomplish it.'" Sarartha Darshini 8.6.15 commentary.

44. "The Lord understood that they were requesting that he give them a method

for regaining Svarga." Sarartha Darshini 8.6.16 commentary.
45. "The real purpose was to get the nectar." SB 8.6.25 purport.
46. "Since they were all becoming tired (Vasuki so much so that he was almost going to die), Lord Visnu, to encourage them to continue the work of churning the ocean, entered into them according to their respective modes of nature…." SB 8.7.11 purport
47. "He entered the Asuras as the energy of rajas… Irayan means 'stimulating'. He entered the devatas as he energy of sattva. He entered Vasuki as the energy of tamas…Due to the illusion created by ignorance, Vasuki would not be conscious of his pain." Sarartha Darshini 8.7.11 commentary.
48. See Sarartha Darshini 8.7.17 verse.
49. "Since Lord Siva is in charge of annihilation, why should he be approached for protection, which is given by Lord Visnu?" SB 8.7.21 purport.
50. "This prayer is actually offered to Lord Vishnu…" SB 8.7.23 purport.
51. "All the ancient Vedic literatures, composed of verses, are your glance." Sarartha Darshini 8.7.30 verse.
52. See SB 8.7.31 purport.
53. "Since the form of Visnu…is the Supreme Brahman, it is not a fault if Visnu does not know this impersonal Brahman belonging to him, since it is like knowledge of a flower in the sky." Sarartha Darshini 8.7.31 commentary.

54. "Kala and Gara were two Asuras that Siva killed...." Sarartha Darshini 8.7.32 commentary.
55. "But you, being an atmarama, should ignore these jivas subjected to mutual hatred in the material world." Sarartha Darshini 8.7.39 commentary.
56. "Durvasa and others cannot control anger. Thus their austerity is useless. Some persons like Brhaspati have knowledge but it is not without material attachment. Thus it is useless. Some like Brahma have great power, but they also have lust." Sarartha Darshini 8.8.20 commentary.
57. "Some, the karmis like Sukracarya, have dharma, but are not friendly to all beings since they are interested in material facility, such as being a priest for Asuras." Sarartha Darshini 8.8.21 commentary.
58. See Sarartha Darshini 8.8.22 commentary.
59. See Sarartha Darshini 8.8.24 commentary.
60. See Sarartha Darshini 8.9.9 commentary.
61. "Therefore, according to Manu-samhita, every woman should be protected, either by her husband, by her father or by her grown sons. Without such protection, a woman will be exploited." SB 8.9.9 purport.
62. Sarartha Darshini 8.9.11 commentary.
63. See purport of SB 8.9.23.
64. "We are now drinking nectar with our ears, eyes and mind. The nectar from the milk ocean cannot be more than this.

What is the use of the nectar? We desire simply to please her." Sarartha Darshini 8.9.21 commentary.
65. See SB 8.10.25 purport.
66. See Sarartha Darshini 8.10.36.
67. "The Lord caught the trident with his left hand as it approached...." Sarartha Darshini 8.10.56 commentary.
68. For Vritrasura's story see Divine Protection (Brilliant as the Sun Canto Six).
69. "If you desire to see the form of Mohini in order to announce to the people your own power of yoga, all this will certainly be revealed to you." Sarartha Darshini 8.12.13 commentary.
70. See SB 8.12.14 purport.
71. "There are fourteen *manvantara-avatāras:* (1) Yajña, (2) Vibhu, (3) Satyasena, (4) Hari, (5) Vaikuṇṭha, (6) Ajita, (7) Vāmana, (8) Sārvabhauma, (9) Ṛṣabha, (10) Viṣvaksena, (11) Dharmasetu, (12) Sudhāmā, (13) Yogeśvara and (14) Bṛhadbhānu. Out of these fourteen *manvantara-avatāras,* Yajña and Vāmana are also *līlā-avatāras.* The *manvantara-avatāras* are also known as *vaibhava-avatāras.*" Teachings of Lord Caitanya chapter 7.
72. See SB 10.84.2-5.
73. SB 10.90.33-34.
74. See SB canto 9, chapter 16 introduction.
75. See The Sages of Naimisharanya, chapter 12.
76. See The Sages of Naimisharanya, chapter 9, texts 40-49.

77. SB 11.8.18 purport.
78. "After assuring the king, Vasiṣṭha spoke with the priests, instructing them to have the sacrificial arena built. Chief among them was Rishwashringa, a powerful Brahmin who had come from the kingdom of Aṅga. It had long ago been prophesied that Rishwashringa would help Daśaratha obtain progeny. Along with Vasiṣṭa, he took charge of the arrangements for the sacrifice." Ramayana, retold by Krishna Dharma, part one, chapter one.
79. See this book, chapter 1 texts 17-18.
80. "This verse describes the action of the sages." Sarartha Darshini 8.14.4 commentary.
81. "'The kings' refers to Manu's sons." Sarartha Darshini 8.14.9 commentary.
82. "All qualities such as fatness and thinness, aging and senility arise from the Lord." Sarartha Darshini 8.14.9 commentary.
83. "This means that though his actions are glorified, the Lord's intention is hard to understand." Sarartha Darshini 8.14.10 commentary.
84. See SB 8.11.46.
85. cf. Krishna Fulfils All Desires, Appendix A.
86. "The sons of Aditi are called Ādityas, and the sons of Diti are called Daityas." Bg 10.30 purport.
87. See Divine Protection 18.47-54.
88. "....the four horns are the four Vedas. The three feet are the three periods of the day. The two heads are the introductory

and concluding portions of sacrifice. The seven hands are seven meters." Sarartha Darshini 8.16.31.
89. See Sarartha Darshini 8.16.33.
90. See Sarartha Darshini 8.16.35.
91. "She saw the Lord as the husband of Laksmi: the Lord could give all wealth to her sons. She saw the Lord as the master of sacrifice, who had appeared because of her vow, which was the essence of all sacrifice. She saw him as the master of the world: by his appearance he would deliver the world." Sarartha Darshini 8.17.7 commentary.
92. Kashyapa fixed the form of the Lord which was within his mind in Aditit's womb by the contact of their bodies." Sarartha Darshini 8.17.23 commentary.
93. "A forest fire begins when two pieces of wood rub against one another, being agitated by the wind. Actually, however, fire belongs neither to the wood nor to the wind; it is always different from both." SB 8.17.23 purport
94. "Lord Kṛṣṇa was first born to Vasudeva and Devakī in their previous lives as Sutapā and Pṛśni. Later they again became His parents as Kaśyapa and Aditi. This, then, was the third time He had appeared as their son." SB 10.85.20 purport.
95. Vamana means 'dwarf' in Sanskrit.
96. See The Science of God, appendix N.
97. "The character of the nihsattva (low person) is that he refuses to give. The krpana is a particular type of ihsattva. He

promises and then does not give." Sarartha Darshini 8.19.3 commentary.

98. "This will be for my hermitage. This will be enough for my subsistence, for I survive by taking whatever food is offered." Sarartha Darshini 8.19.16 commentary.

99. See Krishna Fulfills All Desires, chapters 15-23.

100. See The Universal Order, chapter 15 texts 6-9

101. "One who is not self-controlled, specifically in sex life, can become neither a disciple nor a spiritual master. One must have disciplinary training in controlling speaking, anger, the tongue, the mind, the belly and the genitals. One who has controlled the particular senses mentioned above is called a *gosvāmī*. Without becoming a *gosvāmī* one can become neither a disciple nor a spiritual master." SB 2.9.43 purport.

102. "Tapas means 'concentration of mind' in the context." Sarartha Darshini 8.19.36 commentary.

103. "Charity should be given according to scriptural rules." Sarartha Darshin 8.19.37 commentary.

104. "If I have something to give, and I say I have nothing, how can I avoid the sin of lying?" Sarartha Darshini 8.19.38 commentary.

105. "Similarly, if one does not partake of untruth, the body undoubtedly dies up." Sarartha Darshini 8.19.40 verse.

106. Taken from Sarartha Darshini 8.19.40 commentary
107. See Sarartha Darshini 8.19.42 commentary for the evidence from Sruti.
108. See SB 8.20.6 purport.
109. See SB 8.20.10 purport.
110. "Bali's wife was extremely shy, unexposed even to the sun, but she was unable to conceal her agitation because of joy. She shed tears of joy on understanding the firm bhakti of her husband. Thus ignoring the maidservants, she personally came out of the confines of her room carrying a pot." Sarartha Darshini 8.20.17 commentary.
111. "Bali previously said that he would give Vamana whatever he wanted (SB 8.19.38). Therefore the Lord was free to increase his size to take whatever he wanted." Sarartha Darshini 8.20.21 commentary.
112. Fame, beauty, wisdom, wealth, renunciation, strength.
113. See Mysteries of Creation, Appendix 2.
114. We have more or less copied the translation of this verse as given in Sarartha Darshini 8.20.24.
115. See Sarartha Darshini 8.20.25-29.
116. See the translation in Sarartha Darshini 8.21.2-3.
117. See Srimad Bhagavatam 10.41.44 synonyms
118. See Sarartha Darshini 8.21.8.
119. "Seeing that the Asuras covered with ignorance could not understand philosophy, Bali then gave inspiring

instructions that they could accept." Sarartha Darshini 8.21.23 commentary.
120. "Garuda understood the Lord's intentions. 'Having accepted all of Bali's possessions, my master now desires to accept Bali's very self. Unable to pay his debt, the Lord will become Bali's door keeper. In order to broadcast to the world the Lord's dependence on his devotee and the excellence of his devotee, I will show everyone Bali's indestructible fortitude by punishing him.'" Sarartha Darshini 8.21.26 commentary.
121. "What should I do if I cannot fulfil my promise?" Sarartha Darshini 8.21.32 commentary.
122. "You can ask your learned guru whether what I now say is reasonable or not." Sarartha Darshini 8.21.32 commentary.
123. See SB 8 chapter 22 Introduction.
124. "Do you want to get free of Varuna's ropes and hell?" Sarartha Darshini 8.22.3 commentary.
125. "But your defamation will come from being bound up by me." Sarartha Darshini 8.22.4 commentary.
126. "But I am famous for helping the devatas and not the Asuras." Sarartha Darshini 8.22.5 commentary.
127. "You give us eyes of knowledge; whereas the devatas are blinded." Sarartha Darshini 8.22.5 commentary. See also Bg 13.8-12 which states that humility is the beginning of knowledge.
128. "He was ashamed of being seen by Prahlada, since it would seem that he

must have committed some offense in order to be bound up. Or he was ashamed at seeing Prahlada, since he had suddenly forgotten Prahlada's constant teachins about not showing pride on the occasion of giving land." Sarartha Darshini 8.22.14 commentary.
129. "The Supreme Personality of Godhead is fully independent. Thus it is not always a fact that a living being's loss of all opulence is a sign of the Supreme Lord's mercy upon him. The Lord can act any way He likes. He may take away one's opulence, or He may not." SB 8.22.25 purport
130. "I do not take away his wealth, since there is no harm in his possessing that wealth." Sarartha Darshini 8.22.26 commentary; "Some say that this however is not a fixed rule for the Lord who is skilful at increasing the prema of his devotee. Some give the example of the Lord taking away the wealth of the Pandavas." Sarartha Darshini 8.22.27 commentary.
131. See SB 8.21.34.
132. "One should not say that the devatas will give him trouble in Sutala. He is under my shelter. I will be his door keeper, staying awake all the time to protect him." Sarartha Darshini 8.22.31 commentary. "The Lord was speaking to Brahma. Now he speaks directly to Bali." Sarartha Darshini 8.22.33 commentary.
133. 'What is that result?' Mercy in the form of getting your foot on my head, which is

not attained even by the devatas...." Sarartha Darshini 8.23.2 commentary.
134. See Sarartha Darshini 8.23.8 commentary.
135. "Hari means 'the Lord who takes away the offense of Shukracarya because he was related to Bali." Sarartha Darshini 8.23.13 commentary.
136. See The Universal Order, chapter 18, text 24.
137. "Similarly, when the Supreme Personality of Godhead accepted the abominable form of a fish, He must have done so to favor some devotee. Parīkṣit Mahārāja was eager to know about the devotee for whom the Supreme Lord accepted this form." SB 8.24.2-3 purport.
138. "What is the question of forms like Matsya being superior or inferior since they are *suddha-sattva*?" Sarartha Darshini 8.24.6 commentary.

Glossary

Agni: God of fire, thus also the Sanskrit word for fire.
Anartha: Literally 'unwanted' – impurity of the heart.
Apsara: Celestial nymph of legendary beauty.
Arati: Worship ceremony in which articles like incense, flowers, and fans are offered.
Arghya: Milk-based drink used as a respectful offering made to a guest.
Astra: Divine weapon, usually prefixed by the name of the particular god or force which presides over it; e.g. Brahmastra, a weapon presided over by Lord Brahma.
Asura: Persons possessing an atheistic mentality.
Avadhuta: A saint with no affiliation or attachment to anything material.
Avatar: Appearance of a form of Vishnu within the material world.
Bhairava: Name for Shiva.
Bhava: First stage of love of God.
Brahma: First of the gods and the creator of the universe.
Brahman: The absolute supreme spiritual reality. Krishna's energy.
Brahmin: The priestly class, usually teachers.
Brihaspati: The gods' preceptor.
Chamara: Whisk made from yak-tail hairs and used for highly respectable persons.
Charana: Class of celestials noted for their poetic abilities.
Daitya: Class of powerful demonic beings.
Danava: Class of powerful celestial demons who are the gods' enemies.
Devi: Goddess. Also used as respectful term of address for one's wife.
Dwapara-yuga: Third of the four Vedic ages

Gandharva: Celestial beings famed for their singing and dancing ability, as well as their prowess in battle.
Gandiva: Arjuna's bow.
Garbhodaka: Great ocean filling half of the universe in which lies Garbhodakashayi Vishnu.
Garbhodakashayi Vishnu: Second *Purusha* Avatar or functional incarnation of Vishnu who enters each material universe to facilitate creation.
Gopa: Cowherd man.
Gopi: Cowherd woman.
Indra: King of the gods, also known as Purandara and Shakra.
Japa: Chanting of God's names.
Jaya: Victory or 'All glories'. An exclamation of approval and appreciation.
Jiva: Soul in the material world.
Kali-yuga: Last of the four Vedic ages, also known as the Age of Quarrel and Hypocrisy.
Kalpa: One day of Lord Brahma, or 1000 cycles of the four ages on earth.
Karanodakashayi Vishnu: First *Purusha* Avatar or functional incarnation of Vishnu, also known as Mahavishnu, from whom the universes emanate.
Kauravas: Sons of Dhritarastra.
Kinnara: A class of god, often having a half-human and half- animal form such as that of a centaur, and generally seen holding a lute.
Kirtan: Glorification of Krishna.
Kshatriya: Member of the administrative or ruling class, usually warriors. Considered subordinate to brahmin*s*.
Kshirodakashayi Vishnu: Third *Purusha* Avatar or function incarnation of Vishnu who acts as the Supersoul.
Kusha: *Darbha* grass, considered sacred by the Vedas.

Kuvera: God of wealth, who guards the northern quarter of the universe.
Lokapalas: Gods presiding over the four quarters of the universe.
Mahat-tattva: The total material elements in their non-manifest form.
Makara: Legendary sea creature resembling a huge shark with a crocodile's head.
Maya Danava: A celestial demon possessing great skills at architecture and building.
Manu: Incarnation of Vishnu who rules over mankind.
Naga: Celestial serpent, often appearing in human form.
Naimisharanya: Sacred forest said to be the 'hub' of the universe.
Narada: A celestial sage also known as Devarshi, or the sage among the gods.
Narayana: Name for Vishnu.
Nishadha: Tribal people living in the forest.
Nishtha: Stage of steady practise in *sadhana bhakti*.
Pandavas: Sons of King Pandu.
Parashurama: A sage said to be an empowered incarnation of Vishnu.
Pranayama: A stage of yoga practise where one controls the breathing.
Prema: Pure love for Krishna.
Puranas: Vedic histories, compiled by Vyasadeva.
Rahu: A powerful demon appearing as a shadowy planet.
Rakshasa: Celestial demon, antagonistic to humankind.
Rama: Incarnation of Vishnu, who appeared as a king in the solar dynasty.
Rati: Taste for devotional practise.
Ravana: Powerful leader of the Rakshasa race.

Rishi: Sage.
Rudra: Name for Lord Shiva.
Sadhana: The practises of devotional service.
Sagara: King of the Solar Race. The ocean is also called "*sagara*" as it was the sons of this king who first excavated it.
Sanjivani: Mystical mantra that can bring the dead back to life.
Sankhya: Philosophical process of spiritual advancement which analyses reality.
Satya-yuga: First of the four Vedic ages, also known as the Golden Age.
Shiva: Partial expansion of Vishnu who acts as the universal destroyer at the end of a cycle of ages.
Siddha: Literally, a perfected being. Also a class of gods possessing great mystic powers.
Sita: The daughter of King Janaka who became Rama's wife.
Shudra: Member of the working class who assist the other three classes in society.
Surabhi: A type of celestial cow that gives anything one desires.
Swayamvara: Ceremony where a maiden chooses her own husband.
Timingila: Monstrous aquatic capable of swallowing a whale.
Treta-yuga: Second of the four Vedic ages.
Vaikuntha: The eternal spiritual world.
Vaishya: Member of the productive class, often agriculturalists.
Varna: Vocation.
Varnashrama: Vedic social system of four vocational and four spiritual divisions.
Varuna: God of the waters and the nether worlds.
Vedanta: Short codes compiled by Vyasadeva giving the essence of Vedic knowledge.

Vedas: Ancient Sanskrit scriptures.
Vidhyadhara: A class of god.
Virat Rupa: Universal form of God.
Vishnu: Expansion of Krishna in his role as creator and maintainer of the material world.
Vishnurata: Name for Parikit meaning 'protected by Vishnu.'
Vishvarupa: Universal form of God
Yaksha: Class of gods who are servants of Kuvera.
Yamaduta: Yamaraja's messengers who bring him sinful persons after they die.
Yamaraja: The god who presides over death and destiny. He is empowered by Vishnu to award all beings the results of their actions. He guards the southern quarter of the universe.
Yuga: Vedic age, of which there are four.

About the Authors

Krishna Dharma and his wife Chintamani Dhama Dasi were initiated over 40 years ago into a spiritual lineage that descends from Lord Krishna. Since then, they have been studying and teaching the knowledge of the Vedas and their corollaries, India's ancient Sanskrit classics, primarily Bhagavad-Gita and Srimad Bhagavatam. Krishna Dharma has authored popular retellings of the two great epics, Ramayana and Mahabharata. This is the ninth volume in their *Brilliant as the Sun* series; the previous titles are listed below. They welcome feedback and questions, and can be reached via www.krishnadharma.com, where you will also find details of their other writings.

Other Titles in the Series

Canto One: The Sages of Naimisharanya

The first canto of *Srimad Bhagavatam*. This volume introduces the foundational story; a conversation among many learned sages and yogis at the holy site of Naimisharanya. Five thousand years ago, the world entered the most terrible of the four ages, otherwise known as Kali Yuga, or the 'Age of Quarrel and Hypocrisy'. This era is characterised by terrific acts of violence such as large-scale animal slaughter, systematic destruction of the planet's food supplies, and the merciless affliction of civilian populations by warlords and governments alike. All of this leads to escalating miseries as the dreadful age unfolds. Aware of our impending plight through prophetic visions, the compassionate sages of Naimisharanya seek a way to help us. They question their leader Suta, who has just returned from a quest for solutions. Suta relates what he heard from the great sage Shukadeva as he instructed the world's emperor, Parikit, who had been cursed to die in seven days.

Canto Two: Mysteries of Creation

In this second canto of *Srimad Bhagavatam* we hear the great sage Shukadeva Goswami answering the questions of King Parikit, who has been cursed to die in seven days. After briefly delineating man's highest duty and the best way to conquer suffering and death, Shukadeva explains the path of mystic yoga and meditation. We are then introduced to Lord Brahma, greatest of the gods and engineer of the universe. Questioned by his son Narada, another powerful mystic, he describes the process of creation. We hear how the all-powerful Supreme Person manifests the elements from his spiritual body, enters them, and produces the template for creation which Brahma then effects. 'Mysteries of Creation' presents this profound and illuminating knowledge in a simplified and dramatic style, making it accessible to all.

Canto Three Part One: Vidura's Pilgrimage

In this third canto, we travel with the saint Vidura, of Mahabharata fame, as he meets first with Uddhava, Krishna's secretary and close confidante, and then with the great sage Maitreya. We hear fascinating details about Krishna's divine pastimes and revelations about the cosmos and the nature of time. Replete with powerful mystical teachings spoken by sages and gods, this insightful book will touch your heart and leave you feeling spiritually inspired and renewed.

Canto Three Part Two: Two Avatars

In this second part of canto three, we hear about the appearance of Vishnu's stupendous boar incarnation, Lord Varaha, who rescues the earth from the demon Hiranyaksha. We also meet the great sage Kardama, who marries Devahuti, daughter of the earth's emperor, Manu. She gives birth to Lord Kapila, the divine incarnation who descended to teach the ancient science of Sankhya Yoga. Filled with enlightening wisdom and compelling stories, Two Avataras presents the ancient teachings of the epic Srimad Bhagavatam in a delightful way that will appeal to anyone seeking absolute peace and lasting happiness.

Canto Four: Krishna Fulfils all Desires

In this fourth canto of the *Srimad Bhagavatam,* we hear four vividly recounted histories that show how the Supreme Lord reciprocates with us according to our desire. The first is about Daksha, a celestial progenitor who causes his daughter Sati to give up her life, thus falling foul of her husband, the inscrutable Lord Shiva. The second describes how a five-year-old boy saw God face to face after just six months of spiritual practice. In the third, we meet Prithu, the original king, who confronts the personified Earth when she withholds her produce. The last is a tale of ten princes who set off to perform great penance before ruling the earth and meet Lord Shiva, who teaches them how to achieve life's perfection.

Canto Five: The Universal Order

In this fifth canto, we learn of God's greatness and how his supreme will keeps everything in perfect order. We first meet the powerful King Priyavrata, who rose to the heavens like a second sun to dissipate the darkness of night and create the divisions of Bhumandala. Then comes his son Agnidhra, who weds the celestial beauty Purvachitti and begets on her nine sons, who each become a lord of one province of Jambudvipa, the great earthly island on which we reside. One of those sons, Nabhi, begets Lord Rishabha, the divine incarnation famous for showing the path of Jada-yoga, practised by highly advanced mystics. Rishabha delivers profound spiritual instructions to his hundred sons, the most famous of which was Bharat, after whom the earth was named. We hear how King Bharat somehow fell from the pinnacle of spiritual practice and became a deer in his next life. He then took birth as the self-realised soul, Jada Bharat. In a dialogue of astonishing brilliance, Bharat instructs King Rahugana, laying bare the stark reality of material existence and showing us how to conquer the mind and transcend all suffering. After this, the great sage Shukadeva takes us on a fantastic cosmic journey, revealing the structure and intricacies of the universal planetary systems, from the highest regions of heaven down to the paradisical subterranean provinces of Bila Svarga, homes of the Daityas, Danavas and Nagas—dark beings of phenomenal power. Finally, we hear a harrowing description of the many hells that sinful persons reach, essential reading for anyone who wants to become more serious about his spiritual life.

Canto Six: Divine Protection

In this canto, we see how Krishna saves his devotee from degradation—beginning with the famous story of Ajamila, the brahmin who fell from an exalted position to become a ruthless robber and cheat, only to be miraculously redeemed at the very moment of death. Then we hear how Indra, king of the gods, insulted his guru and, as a result, was overpowered by the demonic races, led by Vritra, a supernatural colossus who had been conjured for the god's destruction. The twist in this tale is that the demon was a great saintly devotee of Krishna. Finally, we hear how Diti, the mother of the demons, gains her salvation. Through all these narrations, we see how, no matter how fallen you are, Krishna will find a way to save you if you have any divine service to your credit.

Canto Seven: The Science of God

In this canto, we first meet Prahlad, a prince in the race of Asuras, fierce enemies of the gods. An exalted saint, he excites the ire of his demonic father Hiranyakshipu by his devotion to Krishna. The demon tries in every way possible to kill his son until at last he is confronted by Krishna's half-man, half-lion incarnation, Nrshinghadeva. After this is a conversation between the celestial sage Narada and King Yudhisthira, in which Narada describes in detail the ancient Vedic system of organizing society known as varnashrama dharma'

Printed in Great Britain
by Amazon